BIBLE CHALLENGE
SHOWDOWN

Goodwin B. Burce

TEACH Services, Inc.
P U B L I S H I N G
www.TEACHServices.com • (800) 367-1844

Copyright © 2017 Goodwin B. Burce
Copyright © 2017 TEACH Services, Inc.
ISBN-13: 978-1-4796-0813-3 (Paperback)
ISBN-13: 978-1-4796-0814-0 (ePub)
ISBN-13: 978-1-4796-0815-7 (Mobi)
Library of Congress Control Number: 2017912257

Published by

TEACH Services, Inc.
PUBLISHING
www.TEACHServices.com • (800) 367-1844

Table of Contents

Foreword

I've known the author of this book, *Bible Challenge Showdown*, personally since he was a little boy. He comes from a very religious Seventh-day Adventist family and thus he has been introduced to the Bible very early in his life. He also attended church school since elementary, and because the Bible was one of the requirements then, the Bible became a part of his life until today. One of the fun youth activities many Seventh-day Adventist churches do is the regular Bible game. Bible games are done in many different ways, from simple race to find a Bible passage to questions about names of people, places, and events. As a child, I always looked forward to Saturday afternoons when we had our usual youth programs and the Bible game was always one of the highlights of the afternoon. I believe that Goodwin Burce had the same experience that I had, and therefore he came up with the idea of writing a book on Bible games. I encourage pastors, youth pastors, church officers, youth leaders, and all church-going persons to get hold of this book, as this can help in your church programs, family time, and even for your personal fun time.

Daniel S. Botabara, D.Min.
Pastor, Central California Conference

Words of Thanks

This book is dedicated to my beloved father who got his daily inspiration from the Bible, even in his sickbed, reading and praying until his final rest.

I first give thanks to God, who gave me life and wisdom, which enables me to do anything at His guidance.

Thanks to Nenita, my wife, who gave me uninterrupted time at my keyboard preparing this book and programming games for the web. Praise God for her full support in publishing this book.

Thanks to Timothy Hullquist and everyone at TEACH Services, Inc., who had everything to do with the publication of this book.

I appreciate everyone for buying this book. I invite you not to just read the Bible at all times, but to:

> Learn it,
> > Understand it, and
> > > Hope to share the wisdom to others.

May you find inspiration and fun from this book and play the game online at http://www.BibleShowdown.com as you study the Bible.

Author's Introduction

Christians read the Holy Bible for many reasons. Some read the Bible to find inspiration to grow their faith. Others read the Bible to understand passages that influence their lives for the better. Whatever their reasons for wanting to know more about the Bible, this book is from God, full of wisdom, inspiration, and truth.

I started reading the Bible at a young age because my parents introduced me to it. The Bible is the book I carry to church. When I started attending church school, reading the Bible became a requirement. Thus the Bible became a part of my life. I became very interested in studying the Bible more when I had a Bible-related discussion with a co-worker. I felt uneasy and uncomfortable answering his questions. I was inspired to read the Bible more and compiled facts from it. To help me learn the facts, I developed Bible quizzes and puzzles. Bible Challenge Showdown is a compilation of Bible facts that simulates the popular Family Feud® game. If you enjoy Bible trivia questions, this book is a fantastic way to test your Bible knowledge and maybe introduce you to some facts you never knew about the scripture before. The subject covers people, places, events, things, and teachings from all sixty-six books of the Old and New Testament. Questions are presented in a fun way in which even kids can learn interesting facts about God's Word.

For everyone who loves a good-natured contest, *Bible Challenge Showdown* has plenty of material to test even the seasoned Bible reader. Beginning Bible students and Bible study groups will also appreciate this book as a quick reference to improve their knowledge. The fun does not end with this book, however. Feel free to play the quiz game online at http://www.BibleShowdown.com where the whole family can enjoy the fun during family game nights.

Goodwin Burce

The Bible

What books of the Old Testament are categorized as the Pentateuch?

Genesis

Exodus

Leviticus

Numbers

Deuteronomy

What books of the Old Testament are categorized as the Narrative Books?

Joshua	2 Kings
Judges	1 Chronicles
Ruth	2 Chronicles
1 Samuel	Ezra
2 Samuel	Nehemiah
1 Kings	Esther

Which books of the Old Testament are named after men?

Joshua	Amos
Ezra	Obadiah
Nehemiah	Jonah
Job	Micah
Solomon	Nahum
Isaiah	Habakkuk
Jeremiah	Zephaniah
Ezekiel	Haggai
Daniel	Zechariah
Hosea	Malachi
Joel	

What Old Testament books are not named after a person?

Lamentations	Proverbs
1 Chronicles	Genesis
2 Chronicles	Exodus
Song of Solomon	Leviticus
1 Kings	Numbers
2 Kings	Deuteronomy
Ecclesiastes	Psalms
Judges	

What are the Minor Prophet books of the Old Testament?

Hosea	Habakkuk
Micah	Obadiah
Joel	Zephaniah
Nahum	Jonah
Amos	Haggai

Who are the New Testament Bible Authors?

James

John

Jude

Luke

Mark

Matthew

Paul

Peter

What books are letters that Paul wrote to individual people?

1 Timothy

2 Timothy

Titus

Philemon

What are the Epistles of Paul?

Romans	1 Timothy
Colossians	2 Timothy
1 Corinthians	Ephesians
2 Corinthians	Titus
1 Thessalonians	Philippians
2 Thessalonians	Philemon
Galatians	

What New Testament Bible books are named after a place or a group of people?

Romans	Galatians
Philippians	Thessalonians
Corinthians	Ephesians
Colossians	Hebrews

What New Testament books are named after men?

Matthew

Titus

Mark

Philemon

Luke

James

John

Peter

Timothy

Jude

Which Bible authors wrote more than one book?

Paul (13)

Moses (6)

John (5)

Samuel (4)

Ezra (4)

Jeremiah (4)

Solomon (3)

Luke (2)

Peter (2)

What books of the Bible have only one chapter?

Obadiah (1)

2 John (1)

3 John (1)

Philemon (1)

Jude (1)

Which Books of the Bible have more than one volume?

Samuel

Thessalonians

Kings

Timothy

Chronicles

Peter

Corinthians

John

What Bible books mentioned/recorded the twelve tribes of Israel?

Genesis (35:22–26)

Judges (5:12–22)

Exodus (1:1–5)

Numbers (1:5–15)

Ezekiel (48:30–34)

Deuteronomy (27:12–13)

1 Chronicles (12:24–38)

Revelation (7:5–8)

Joshua (21:4–8)

What Bible books mention "a land flowing with milk and honey?"

Exodus (3:8)

Joshua (5:6)

Leviticus (20:24)

Jeremiah (11:5)

Numbers (13:27)

Ezekiel (20:6)

Deuteronomy (11:9)

Which Bible writers mention that The Lord "is slow to anger?"

Nehemiah (Neh. 9:17)

David (Ps. 103:8)

Joel (Joel 2:13)

Jonah (Jonah 4:2)

Nahum (Nahum 1:3)

Which Bible writers mention hell?

Moses (Deut. 32:22)

Isaiah (Isa. 5:14)

Samuel (2 Sam. 22:6)

Ezekiel (Ezek. 32:21)

Job (Job 11:8)

Amos (Amos 9:2)

David (Ps. 9:17)

Jonah (Jonah 2:2)

Solomon (Prov. 15:11)

Habakkuk (Hab. 2:5)

Which Bible authors mention leopards in their book?

Solomon (Song of Sol. 4:8)

Hosea (Hos. 13:7)

Isaiah (Isa. 11:6)

Habakkuk (Hab. 1:8)

Jeremiah (Jer. 13:23)

John (Rev. 13:2)

Daniel (Dan. 7:6)

In what books of the Bible are bears mentioned?

   1 Samuel (17:34)
   2 Samuel (17:8)
   2 Kings (2:24)
   Proverbs (28:15)
   Isaiah (11:7)
   Lamentations (3:10)
   Daniel (7:5)
   Hosea (13:8)
   Amos (5:19)
   Revelation (13:2)

Which Old Testament writers mention a "yoke?"

   Moses (Lev. 26:13)
   Samuel (1 Sam. 6:7)
   Ezra (2 Chron. 10:4)
   Isaiah (Isa. 9:4)
   Jeremiah (Jer. 2:20)
   Ezekiel (Ezek. 34:27)
   Hosea (Hosea 11:4)
   Nahum (Nahum 1:13)

In what verses can you find: "O give thanks unto the Lord; for he is good; for his mercy endureth for ever?"

   1 Chronicles 16:34
   Psalm 106:1
   Psalm 107:1
   Psalm 118:1
   Psalm 118:29
   Psalm 136:1

What are other professions of Bible Writers?
Shepherd—Moses, David (1 Sam.17:34)
Cupbearer—Nehemiah (Neh. 1:11)
Priest—Ezekiel (Ezek. 1:3)
Messenger of God—Isaiah (Isa. 42:1)
Scribe—Ezra (Neh. 8:1)
Tax collector—Matthew (Matt. 9:9)
Physician—Luke (Col. 4:14)
Fisherman—John, Peter (Matt. 4:18–22)
Pharisee/Prosecutor—Paul (Acts 8:1–3)
Commander of Israel—Moses, Joshua (Exod. 17:8–16)
Adviser of the King—Daniel (Dan. 2)
King of Israel—David, Solomon (2 Sam. 2:4)
Leader of Israel—Joshua (Joshua 1)
Prophet of God—Isaiah, Jeremiah, others (2 Kings 19:2)
Preacher of God—Paul, all disciples (Acts 15:35)

What books of people or records of people are mentioned in other books of the Bible but did not become an official Bible book?
Book of the Generations of Adam (Gen. 5:1)
Book of Shemaiah the prophet (2 Chron. 12:15)
Book of Jasher (Joshua 10:13)
Book of Jehu the son of Hanani (2 Chron. 20:34)
Book of the Acts of Solomon (1 Kings 11:41)
Book of Moses (2 Chron. 35:12)
Book of Nathan the prophet (1 Chron. 29:29)
Book of the Purchase (Jer. 32:12)
Book of Gad the seer (1 Chron. 29:29)
Book of the generation of Jesus Christ (Matt. 1:1)

What non-personal books of record are mentioned in other books of the Bible but did not become an official Bible book?

    Book of the Covenant (Exod. 24:7)

    Book of the Chronicles of the Kings of Judah (1 Kings 14:29)

    Book of the Wars of the Lord (Num. 21:14)

    Book of Chronicles of the Kings of Media and Persia (Esther 10:2)

    Book of the Law of Moses (Joshua 8:31)

    Book of the Living (Ps. 69:28)

    Book of the Law of God (Joshua 24:26)

    Book of Remembrance (Mal. 3:16)

    Book of the Chronicles of the Kings of Israel (1 Kings 14:19)

    Book of Life (Phil. 4:3)

Fill in the blank: "Bread of _____"

Thy God (Lev. 21:8)

Heaven (Ps. 105:40)

Firstfruits (Lev. 23:20)

Him with an evil eye (Prov. 23:6)

Land (Num. 15:19)

Mourners (Hosea 9:4)

Provision (Joshua 9:5)

Increase of the earth (Isa. 30:23)

Governor (Neh. 5:14)

Of men (Ezek. 24:17)

Affliction (Deut. 16:3)

Idleness (Prov. 31:27)

Tears (Ps. 80:5)

Adversity (Isa. 30:20)

Sorrows (Ps. 127:2)

Life (John 6:35)

Wickedness (Prov. 4:17)

Sincerity and truth (1 Cor. 5:8)

Deceit (Prov. 20:17)

What natural objects are used as symbols in Bible Prophecy?

Water (Holy Spirit / Everlasting Life, John 4:14, Eph. 5:26)

Waters (Inhabited area/people, nations, Rev. 17:15)

Fire (Holy Spirit, Luke 3:16)

Tree (Cross; People/Nation, Deut. 21:22–23, Ps. 92:12, 37:35)

Fig Tree (A Nation that should bear fruit, Luke 13:6–9)

Vineyard (Church that should bear fruit, Luke 20:9–16)

Seed (Descendants/Jesus, Romans 9:8, Gal. 3:16)

Fruit (Works/Actions, Gal. 5:22)

Reapers (Angels, Matt. 13:39)

Thorns/Thorny Ground (Cares of this life, Mark 4:18–19)

Stars (Angels/messengers, Rev. 1:16, 20; Job 38:7)

Sun (Jesus/the gospel, Ps. 84:11; Mal. 4:2; Matt. 17:2)

Mountains (Political or religio-political powers, Isa. 2:2–3;
Jer. 17:3, 25; Ezek. 17:22; Dan. 2:35)

Field (World, Matt. 13:38, John 4:35)

Rock (Jesus/truth, 1 Cor. 10:4; Isa. 8:13, 14; Rom. 9:33; Matt. 7:24)

Winds (Strife/commotion/"winds of war", Jer. 49:36–37; Zech. 7:14)

Finish the following verses from Psalms 150 (NIV): "Praise the Lord…"

… in his sanctuary

… with the harp and lyre

… in his mighty heavens

… with timbrel and dancing

… for his acts of power

… with the strings and pipe

… for his surpassing greatness

… with the clash of cymbals

… with the sounding of the trumpet

… with resounding cymbals

Fill in the blank: "The Word of the Lord is..."

    Tried (2 Sam. 22:31)

    Right (Ps. 33:4)

    Truth (1 Kings 17:24)

    A reproach (Jer. 6:10)

    With Him (2 Kings 3:12)

    Endureth forever, (1 Peter 1:25)

    Pure (Ps. 12:6)

What does the Bible say of a False Witness?

    A false witness testifies against (Deut. 19:16)

    A false witness speaketh lies (Prov. 6:19)

    A false witness soweth discord among brethren (Prov. 6:19)

    A false witness is deceit (Prov. 12:17)

    A false witness shall perish (Prov.21:28)

What physical sicknesses are mentioned in the Bible?

    Atrophy (Job 16:8)

    Dysentery/Worms (2 Chron. 21:12–19)

    Blindness (Job 29:15)

    Fever (Deut. 28:22)

    Deafness (Psalms 38:13)

    Issue of Blood (Matt. 9:20)

    Dropsy (Luke 14:2)

    Lameness (2 Sam. 4:4)

    Dumbness (Prov. 31:8)

    Palsy (Matt. 8:6)

What skin diseases are mentioned in the Scripture?
Boils (Exod. 9:10)
Wounds (Isa. 1:6)
Bruises (Isa. 1:6)
Putrifying sores (Isa. 1:6)
Leprosy (Lev. 13:2)
Emerods (Deut. 28:27)
Itch (Deut. 28:27)
Scab (Deut. 28:27)
Stroke of a wound (Isaiah 30:26)

According to 2 Corinthians 11:26, from what was Paul in danger?
Rivers/Waters
City
Bandits/Robbers
Wilderness/Country
Countrymen/Jews
Sea
Gentiles
False brothers

What are the parts of his body that Job mentions?
Head (Job 29:3)
Face (Job 30:10)
Right hand (Job 30:12)
Feet (Job 30:12)
Skin (Job 30:30)
Eyes (Job 31:1)
Arm (Job 31:22)
Shoulder (Job 31:22)
Mouth/lips (Job 31:27)
Bosom/belly (Job 31:33)

What things mentioned in Romans 8:35–39 cannot separate us from the love of Christ?

Tribulation, Distress

Death, Life

Persecution, Sword

Angels, other creatures

Famine

Principalities, Powers

Nakedness

Things present, Things to come

Peril

Height, depth

What languages or peoples were heard and understood at Pentecost according to Acts 2:8–11?

Parthians	Rome
Medes	Pontus
Egypt	Asia
Elamites	Jews
Mesopotamia	proselytes
Libya	Phrygia
Judaea	Pamphylia
Cappadocia	Cretes
Cyrene	Arabians

What things were mentioned in the Bible as "White as Snow?"

Miriam's leprous skin (Num. 12:10)

Naaman's leprous skin (2 Kings 5:27)

Scattered Kings (Ps. 68:14)

Sins (Isa. 1:18)

Ancient of Days' Garment (Dan. 7:9)

Angel's raiment at Jesus' tomb (Matt. 28:3)

Jesus' raiment at transfiguration (Mark 9:3)

Head and Hair of the Son of Man (Rev. 1:14)

Who were the enemies of Israel according to Judges 3:1–6?

Amorites

Jebusites

Canaanites

Perizzites

Hittites

Philistines

Hivites

Sidonians

The Bible mentions what notable points in regards to Noah?

Found grace in the eyes of the Lord (Gen. 6:8)

A just man (Gen. 6:9)

Perfect in his generations (Gen. 6:9)

Walked with God (Gen. 6:9)

Obedient for he did according unto all the Lord commanded him (Gen. 7:5)

God blessed Noah and his sons (Gen. 9:1)

God establish covenant with him and his seed (Gen. 9:8, 9)

Habakkuk said in Habakkuk 3:17–19 to rejoice always in the Lord, even when…

The fig tree shall not blossom

Fields shall yield no meat

Fruit shall not be in the vines

Flock shall be cut off from the fold

Labour of the olive shall fail

There shall be no herd in the stalls

Fill in the blank: The "way of the wicked…"

… he turneth upside down (Ps. 146:9)

… is as darkness (Prov. 4:19)

… seduceth them (Prov. 12:26)

… is an abomination unto the LORD (Prov. 15:9)

… [why does it] prosper? Jer. 12:1

What should you do "with all your heart?"

Love the Lord your God (Deut. 11:13)

Seek the Lord (2 Chron. 22:9)

Serve the Lord in truth (1 Sam. 12:20, 24)

Seek his God (2 Chron. 31:21)

Follow Me (1 Kings 14:8)

Keep His commandments and testimonies (2 Chron. 34:31)

Turn to the Lord (2 Kings 23:25)

According to Ephesians 4:4–6, what Paul's seven uniting "ONES?"

Body

Faith

Spirit

Baptism

Hope

God and Father

Lord

What were the ten plagues God sent to Egypt? Exodus 7–11

Water to Blood	Locusts
Boils	Flies
Frogs	Darkness
Thunder and Hail	Diseased livestock
Gnats or Lice	Death of Firstborn

What are the colors of the Four Horses of Prophecy that John saw and recorded in Revelation? Revelation 6:2–8

White

Red

Black

Pale Green

When two men are specifically mentioned in the Bible, what are they doing?

Stayed with Lot (Gen. 19:1)

Hid in the roof (Joshua 2:4)

Accompanied Abraham to offer Isaac (Gen. 22:3)

Bear witness against Naboth (1 Kings 21:10)

Fighting (Exod. 2:13)

Received gift from Naaman for Gehazi (2 Kings 5:22)

Prophesied in the camp (Eldad and Medad) (Num. 11:26)

Followed Jesus, cried "have mercy" (Matt. 9:27)

Spied out Jericho (Joshua 2:1)

Sitting by the way side (Matt. 20:30)

What gifts did Jacob prepare for the man, Joseph? (Genesis 43:10–12)

Best fruit of the land

Myrrh

Little balm

Nuts

Little honey

Almonds

Spices

Money

What offending body parts are to be cut off to be saved from hell fire?

Eye (Matt. 5:29)

Foot (Mark 9:45)

Hand (Matt. 5:30)

Tongue (James 3:6)

Soul (Acts 2:27)

What does the Bible compare the tongue to?

Tongue deviseth mischiefs like a sharp razor (Ps. 52:2)

Whet their tongue like a sword (Ps. 64:3)

Sharpened their tongues like a serpent (Ps. 140:3)

Bend their tongues like their bow for lies (Jer. 9:3)

Cloven tongues like as of fire (Acts 2:3)

What did David say about lips in Psalms?

Lord shall cut off all flattering lips (Ps. 12:3)

Let the lying lips be put to silence (Ps. 31:18)

Keep thy lips from speaking guile (Ps. 34:13)

Grace is poured into thy lips (Ps. 45:2)

My lips shall praise thee, because thy lovingkindness is better than life (Ps. 63:3)

My mouth shall praise thee with joyful lips (Ps. 63:5)

My lips shall greatly rejoice when I sing unto thee (Ps. 71:23)

My lips shall utter praise (Ps. 119:171)

Deliver my soul, O Lord, from lying lips (Ps. 120:2)

Let the mischief of their own lips cover them (Ps. 140:9)

What negative things does Proverbs say about lips?

Flattering of her lips she forced him (Prov. 7:21)

Lips are the snare of his soul (Prov. 18:7)

Wickedness is an abomination to my lips (Prov. 8:7)

Perverse in his lips is a fool (Prov. 19:1)

Lying lips are abomination to the Lord (Prov. 12:22)

Meddle not with him that flattereth with his lips (Prov. 20:19)

Openeth wide his lips shall have destruction (Prov. 13:3)

Lips talk of mischief/destruction (Prov. 24:2)

A fool's lips enter into contention (Prov. 18:6)

What positive things does Proverbs say about lips?

Lips may keep knowledge (Prov. 5:2)

Lips speak of excellent/right things (Prov. 8:6)

But he that refraineth his lips is wise (Prov. 10:19)

Lips of the righteous feed many (Prov. 10:21)

Lips of the righteous know what is acceptable (Prov. 10:32)

Lips of the wise shall preserve them (Prov. 14:3)

Lips of the wise disperse knowledge (Prov. 15:7)

Righteous lips are the delight of kings (Prov. 16:13)

Sweetness of the lips increaseth learning (Prov. 16:21)

Lips of knowledge are a precious jewel (Prov. 20:15)

What does God do for the widows?

Surely hears their cry (Exod. 22:22, 23)

Judges (Deut. 10:18)

Relieves (Ps. 146:9)

Establishes the border (Prov. 15:25)

Will witness against oppressors (Mal. 3:5)

What blessings does God promise Isaac? Genesis 26:3–5

I will be with you

I will give you all these lands

I will make your descendants multiply as the stars of heaven

In your seed, all nations of the earth will be blessed

What promises does Ishmael receive from God? Genesis 16:10–12

Be a wild man

His hand shall be against every man

Every man's hand will be against him

He will dwell in the presence of all his brethren

What promises does Esau receive from God? Genesis 27:39–40

    Dwell in the fatness of the earth with the dew of heaven

    Live by his sword

    Serve his brother (*Jacob*)

    Have his own dominion

    Break his yoke from his neck

What blessings does Jacob receive from his father, Isaac?
Genesis 27:27–29

    May the Lord give you of the dew of heaven

    Be master over your brethren

    Fatness of the earth

    Let your mother's sons bow down to you

    Plenty of corn and wine

    Cursed be everyone who curses you

    Let people serve you

    Blessed be those who bless you

    Many nations will bow down to you

What was John the Baptist's response when people asked, "What shall we do?" Luke 3:11–14

    He who has two tunics, let him give to him who has none

    He who has food, let him give to him who has none

    Collect no more than what is appointed for you

    Do not intimidate anyone

    Do not accuse falsely

    Be content with your wages

Fill in the blank: Job acknowledges that "I am____" what?
... a burden to myself (Job 7:20)
... afraid of all my sorrows (Job 9:28)
... full of confusion (Job 10:15)
... one mocked of his neighbor (Job 12:4)
... an alien in their sight (Job 19:15)
... their byword (Job 30:9)
... become like dust and ashes (Job 30:19)
... a brother to dragons and a companion to owls (Job 30:29)
... innocent, righteous (Job 33:9)
... vile (Job 40:4)

What groups of people were present at the dedication of the image of Nebuchadnezzar? Daniel 3:2, 8

Princes	Rulers
Counselors	Judges
Governors	Chaldeans
Sheriffs	Treasurers
Captains	Jews

According to Solomon, "The Fear of the Lord" is what?
... is to hate evil ways (Prov. 8:13)
... is the beginning of wisdom (Prov. 9:10)
... prolongeth days (Prov. 10:27)
... is strong confidence (Prov. 14:26)
... is a fountain of life (Prov. 14:27)
... is better than great treasure and trouble therewith (Prov. 15:16)
... is the instruction of wisdom (Prov. 15:33)
... men depart from evil (Prov. 16:6)
... tendeth to life (Prov. 19:23)
... riches, and honour, and life (Prov. 22:4)

Fill in the blank with a person's name: "Spirit of ..."
Spirit of Jacob (Gen. 45:27)
Spirit of Pul king of Assyria (1 Chron. 5:26)
Spirit of Tilgathpilneser, king of Assyria (1 Chron. 5:26)
Spirit of Cyrus king of Persia (2 Chron. 36:22)
Spirit of Elijah (2 Kings 2:15)
Spirit of Zerubbabel the son of Shealtiel (Hag. 1:14)
Spirit of Joshua the son of Josedech (Hag. 1:14)

Fill in the blank with a name of a group or type of people: "Spirit of ..."
Spirit of the Philistines (2 Chron. 21:16)
Spirits of all flesh (Num. 16:22)
Spirit of princes (Ps. 76:12)
Spirit of a man (Prov. 18:14)
Spirit of the ruler (Eccl. 10:4)
Spirit of the kings of the Medes (Jer. 51:11)
Spirit of all the remnant of the people (Hag. 1:14)
Spirits of just men (Heb. 12:23)

Fill in the blank with an activity: "Spirit of ..."
Spirit of deep sleep/slumber (Isa. 29:10; Rom. 11:8)
Spirit of whoredoms (Hosea 4:12)
Spirit of adoption (Rom. 8:15)
Spirit of promise (Eph. 1:13)
Spirit of error (1 John 4:6)

All scripture is inspiration of God, and is profitable for what? 2 Timothy 3:16
Doctrine
Reproof
Correction
Instruction

Fill in the blank: "The Law is made for..."? 1 Timothy 1:8–10

Lawless and disobedient

Whoremongers

Ungodly and for sinners

Menstealers

Unholy and profane

Liars

Murderers of fathers and mothers

Perjured persons

Manslayers

Anything contrary to sound doctrine

To which groups did the Bible say: "Woe Unto You?"

...those that desire the day of the Lord (Amos 5:18)

...those that laugh now (Luke 6:25)

...ye blind guides (Matt. 23:16)

...when all men shall speak well of you (Luke 6:26)

...those that are rich (Luke 6:24)

...ye lawyers (Luke 11:46, 52)

...those that are full (Luke 6:25)

...ye who build the sepulchers of the prophets (Luke 11:47)

Who is the Bible talking about when it says, "thou shalt not uncover the nakedness?"

Thy Mother ("thy father's wife") (Lev. 18:8)

Thy Sister (Lev. 18:11)

Thy Aunt (Lev. 18:14)

Daughter-in-law (Lev. 18:15)

Sister-in-law (Lev. 18:16)

Neighbour's wife (Lev. 18:20)

God, Jesus and Holy Spirit

How is God referred to as a "rock" in the Bible?

He is the Rock, His work is perfect (Deut. 32:4)

The Lord is my rock, and my fortress (2 Sam. 22:2–3)

The God of my rock; in Him will I trust (2 Sam. 22:2–3)

The Lord liveth; and blessed be my rock (2 Sam. 22:47)

God of the rock of my salvation (2 Sam. 22:47)

O Lord my rock; be not silent to me (Ps. 28:1)

Be thou my strong rock, (Ps. 31:2)

Lead me to the rock that is higher than I (Ps. 61:2)

The rock of my strength, and my refuge (Ps. 62:6–7)

Lord is my defence; God is the rock of my refuge (Ps. 94:22)

What symbols does the Bible use to describe the Holy Spirit?

Still small voice
  (1 Kings 19:11–13)

Wind (Acts 2:2)

Fire (Acts 2:2, 3; Isa. 4:4)

Dove (Luke 3:22)

Water (John 7:37–39)

Anointing oil (Acts 10:38)

In what events is the appearance of a rainbow recorded in the Bible?

A sign of Covenant between God and the earth and every living
creature (Gen. 9:13, 16)

At the throne of God in Ezekiel's vision (Ezek. 1:28)

Around God's throne in heaven in John's vision (Rev. 4:3)

On the head of a mighty angel coming down from heaven
(Rev. 10:1)

Fill in the blank from Isaiah: "I am the Lord…"

…that is My name (Isa. 42:8)

…there is none else (Isa. 45:5)

…the Holy One of Israel (Isa. 43:3)

…which teacheth thee to profit (Isa. 48:17)

…beside Me there is no Savior (Isa. 43:11)

…they shall not be ashamed (Isa. 49:23)

…the creator of Israel (Isa. 43:15)

…that divided the sea (Isa. 51:15)

…that maketh all things (Isa. 44:24)

How does the Bible compare the Lord God to fire?

Sight of the glory of the Lord was like devouring fire (Exod. 24:17)

Presence of Lord thy God is as a consuming fire (Deut. 9:3)

His jealousy burns like fire (Ps. 79:5)

His wrath burns like fire (Ps. 89:46)

His tongue is as a devouring fire (Isa. 30:27)

His Fury comes forth like fire (Jer. 4:4)

His word was in mine heart as a burning fire shut up in my bones
(Jer. 20:9)

His eyes were as a flame of fire (Rev. 19:12)

What are some of the Lord's attributes, other than "slow to anger?"

Ready to pardon (Neh. 9:17)

Merciful (Neh. 9:17)

Gracious (Neh. 9:17)

Great kindness (Joel 2:13)

Repenteth him of evil (Joel 2:13)

Great in power (Nahum 1:3)

Full of compassion (Ps. 145:8)

What makes the Psalmist say, "God's mercy endures forever?"
Psalms 136:1–14

Give thanks for He is good

He made the sun, moon, and stars

Give thanks to God of gods

Smote Egyptian firstborn

Who alone do great wonders

Brought Israel out from Egypt

His wisdom made the heavens

Divided the Red Sea

Stretched out the earth above waters

Made Israel pass through midst of it

Overthrew Pharaoh's host at the Red Sea

Remembered us in our low estate

Led His people through wilderness

Redeemed us from our enemies

Smote great and famous kings

Giveth food to all flesh

Gave land for an heritage to Israel

Give thanks unto the God of heaven

What are descriptions of the Lord God according to Moses and David?

Merciful (Exod. 34:6–7)

Gracious (Exod. 34:6–7)

Longsuffering (Exod. 34:6–7)

Abundant in Goodness (Exod. 34:6–7)

Truthful (Exod. 34:6–7)

Righteous, Upright (Ps. 145:17)

Great God (Ps. 95:3)

Slow to Anger (Ps. 103:8)

Our Defence (Ps. 89:18)

Our Keeper (Ps.121:5)

According to David, "THE LORD IS MY...?"

... Rock (Ps.18:2)

... Buckler (Ps.18:2)

... Fortress (Ps. 18:2)

... Deliverer (Ps. 18:2)

... God (Ps. 18:2)

... Refuge (Ps. 94:22)

... Defence (Ps.94:22)

... Strength (Ps. 28:7)

... Shield (Ps. 28:7)

... Shepherd (Ps. 23:1)

... Light (Ps. 27:1)

Fill in the blank: David said of the Lord, "Thy right hand..."

Shall teach thee (Ps. 45:4)

Shall save me (Ps. 138:7)

Save and hear me (Ps. 60:5)

Lead and hold me (Ps. 139:10)

Upholdeth me (Ps. 63:8)

[is] high (Ps. 89:13)

According to David, what benefits are there in "trust*(ing)* in the Lord?"

Save me from all that persecute me (Ps. 7:1)

My refuge and my fortress (Ps. 91:2)

He is a bucker to all those that trust (Ps. 18:30)

Shall not be afraid of evil tidings (Ps. 112:7)

Shall dwell in the land and be fed (Ps. 37:3)

He is their help and their shield (Ps. 115:9)

Deliver from the wicked and be save (Ps. 37:40)

Shall be as Mt. Zion, which cannot be removed (Ps. 125:1)

Never be put to confusion (Ps. 71:1)

Leave not my soul destitute (Ps. 141:8)

What benefits are there for those who "wait upon the Lord?"

He shall strengthen thine heart (Ps. 27:14)

Until that he have mercy upon us (Ps. 123:2)

Prospereth in his way (Ps. 37:7)

He shall save thee (Prov. 20:22)

They shall inherit the land/earth (Ps. 37:9)

They shall run, and not be weary; walk, and not faint (Isa. 40:31)

God is my defence (Ps. 59:9)

The Lord is good unto them (Lam. 3:25)

From Him cometh my salvation (Ps. 62:1)

My God will hear me (Micah 7:7)

What is promised for those [who] "trust*(ing)* in the Lord?"

He will deliver thee (2 Kings 18:30)

He is their help and shield (Ps. 115:10)

He is a buckler to all (2 Sam. 22:31)

Happy is he (Prov. 16:20)

Be blessed (Ps. 34:8)

Shall be made fat (prosper) (Prov. 28:25)

Mercy shall encompass him (Ps. 32:10)

Shall be safe (Prov. 29:25)

Thou art my hope (Ps. 71:5)

Is everlasting strength (Isa. 26:4)

Finish the verse: The "Right Hand" of the Lord (is) …

Glorious in power dashes the enemy in pieces (Exod. 15:6)

Holden me up (Ps. 18:35)

Stretchedst out and earth swallowed them (Exod. 15:12)

Shall find out those that hate thee (Ps. 21:8)

Fiery law for the thousands of saints (Deut. 33:2)

Doeth valiantly (Ps. 118:15)

Joy and pleasure for evermore (Ps. 16:11)

Keeper and shade (Ps. 121:5)

Savest them that trust Thee (Ps. 17:7)

Full of righteousness (Ps. 48:10)

Finish the verse: "The Voice of the Lord is…"

Upon the waters (Ps. 29:3)

Powerful (Ps. 29:4)

Full of majesty (Ps. 29:4)

Breaketh the cedars of Lebanon (Ps. 29:5)

Divideth the flames of fire (Ps. 29:7)

Shaketh the wilderness of Kadesh (Ps. 29:8)

Maketh the hinds to calve (Ps. 29:9)

Discovereth the forests (Ps. 29:9)

Everyone in His temple speaks of His glory (Ps. 29:9)

What happens if ye will not obey or hear the "Voice of the Lord?"

Ye shall perish (Deut. 8:20)

Curses shall come upon thee (Deut. 28:15)

Ye shall be few in numbers (Deut. 28:62)

Ye shall not prolong your days upon the land (Deut. 30:18)

Hand of the Lord shall be against you (1 Sam. 12:15)

Lord would not shew them the land that floweth with milk and honey (Joshua 5:6)

What are the consequences of God's judgment on the Philistines?
Zepheniah 2:1–7

> Gaza and Ashkelon will be deserted and left in ruins.
>
> Ashdod will be emptied in broad daylight, and Ekron uprooted.
>
> "I am now your enemy, and I'll wipe you out."
>
> Your seacoast will be changed into pastureland and sheep pens.
>
> Survivors in Judah will take your land to use for pasture.
>
> And when evening comes, Judah will rest in houses at Ashkelon.

What are God's judgments on Assyria? Zepheniah 2:13–15

> He will stretch out His hand against the north, destroy Assyria.
>
> Make Nineveh a desolation, as dry as the wilderness.
>
> The herds shall lie down in her midst, every beast of the nation.
>
> Both the pelican and the bittern shall lodge on the capitals
>   of her pillars.
>
> Their voice shall sing in the windows.
>
> Desolation shall be at the threshold.
>
> He will lay bare the cedar work.
>
> Everyone who passes by her shall hiss and shake his fist.

What does the Bible mean by "walk in all His (God) ways?"

> Keep mine ordinances (Lev. 18:4)
>
> Keep the commandments (Deut. 8:6)
>
> Fear the Lord thy God (Deut. 10:12)
>
> Love the Lord your God to cleave unto Him (Deut. 11:22)
>
> Keep His statutes (Deut. 26:17)
>
> Serve Him with all your heart and soul (Joshua 22:5)
>
> Keep His judgments and His testimonies (1 Kings 2:3)
>
> Obey My voice (Jer. 7:23)
>
> Do justly, and to love mercy (Micah 6:8)
>
> Being fruitful in every good work, and increasing in the knowledge
>   of God (Col. 1:10)

What words does Moses use to describe the Lord God? Exodus 34:6–7

Merciful

Gracious

Longsuffering

Abundant in Goodness and Truth

Keeping mercy for thousands

Forgiving iniquity and transgression, sin

Finish the verse; "God is my…"

… strength (2 Sam. 22:33)

… power (2 Sam. 22:33)

… glory (Ps. 62:7)

… King (Ps. 74:12)

… defence (Ps. 59:9, 17)

… witness (Rom. 1:9)

… salvation (Ps. 62:7)

… record (Phil. 1:8)

Fill in the blanks from Psalms: "The _____ of the Lord is _____"

Word … tried (Ps. 18:30)

Law … perfect (Ps. 19:7)

Testimony … sure (Ps. 19:7)

Statutes … right (Ps. 19:8)

Commandment … pure (Ps. 19:8)

Fear … clean (Ps. 19:9)

Judgments … true and righteous (Ps. 19:9)

Voice … powerful, full of majesty (Ps. 29:4)

Face … against them that do evil (Ps. 34:16)

Mercy … from everlasting to everlasting (Ps. 103:17)

What great things did God do at night?

Lord passed over Egypt (Exod. 12:12)

God brought Israel out of Egypt (Exod. 12:42)

Pillar of Fire to Israelites (Exod. 13:21)

Divided the water and made the Red Sea dry land (Exod. 14:21)

Manna fell upon the camp (Num. 11:9)

Dew on the ground, fleece was dry (Judges 6:40)

Jesus walked on the sea (Matt. 14:25)

Conversion of Nicodemus (John 3:2)

Jesus prays in the mountain (Luke 6:12)

Peter and apostles delivered from prison (Acts 5:19)

What are the petitions in the Lord's Prayer? Matthew 6:9–13

Hallowed be thy name

Thy kingdom come

Thy will be done in earth, as it is in heaven

Give us this day our daily bread

Forgive us our debts, as we forgive our debtors

Lead us not into temptation

Deliver us from evil

In what unique ways does God allow the Israelites to know Him?
Deuteronomy 4:34

By temptations

By a mighty hand

By signs

By a stretched-out arm

By wonders

By great terrors

By war

What happens if thou will not "seek the Lord God?"
    He will cast thee off forever (1 Chron. 28:9)
    Shall be put to death (2 Chron. 15:13)
    He will forsake you (2 Chron. 15:2)
    His power and His wrath is against them (Ezra 8:22)
    Salvation is far from the wicked (Ps. 119:155)

What were the seven last statements of Jesus Christ?
    Father, forgive them; for they know not what they do (Luke 23:34)
    Today shalt thou be with me in paradise (Luke 23:43)
    Behold thy mother (John 19:27)
    Eloi, Eloi, lama sabachthani? My God, My God, why have You
       forsaken Me? (Mark 15:34)
    I thirst (John 19:28)
    It is finished (John 19:30)
    Father, into Thy hands I commend My spirit (Luke 23:46)

Finish the verse: Jesus said, "I AM THE…"
    … bread of life (John 6:35)
    … resurrection and life (John 11:25)
    … living bread came down from heaven (John 6:41)
    … way, truth, and the life (John 14:6)
    … light of the world (John 8:12)
    … true vine (John 15:1)
    … door/gate of the sheep (John 10:7)
    … good shepherd (John 10:11)
    … Alpha and Omega, the first and the last (Rev. 1:11)
    … root and offspring of David (Rev. 22:16)

What mocking words were said of Jesus while on the cross?
Matthew 27:39–43

> Thou destroyest and buildest the temple in three days; save thyself.
>
> If thou be the Son of God, come down from the cross.
>
> He saved others; himself he cannot save.
>
> If he be the King of Israel, let him now come down from the cross, and we will believe him.
>
> He trusted in God; let Him deliver him now.

What things were done to Jesus Christ before and during His crucifixion?

Lacerated His head (Matt. 27:29)

Spat in His face (Matt. 27:30)

Buffeted His cheeks (Matt. 26:67)

Plucked off His beard (Isaiah 50:6)

Bound Him and nailed His feet (Mark 15:1, 24)

Speared His side/Scourged His body (Matt. 27:26)

Stripped His body/Took away His garments (Matt. 27:28)

Mocked His person/Lied about Him (Matt. 27:29–39)

False witnesses lied about Him (Matt. 26:60–61)

Condemned Him unjustly (Luke 23:41)

Denied His mission/Taunted His works (Mark 14:29–30; 15:31)

What did Christ suffer to His body?

His face was marred (Mark 14:65)

His hands were nailed to the cross (Luke 24:39)

His back was lacerated (Mark 15:15)

His feet were torn (Ps. 22: 16)

His brow was scarred (Matt. 27:29)

His body was exposed to the unholy gaze of mob (Matt. 27:36–42)

His side was pierced (John 19:34)

Over what did Christ have authority in the Bible?

Authority over sickness (Mark 3:15)

Authority to lay down his life (John 10:18–19)

Authority to judge (John 5:27)

Authority to forgive sins (Matt. 9:6–8)

Authority over all men (John 17:2)

Authority over demons/Unclean Spirits (Mark 1:27)

Authority in heaven and earth (Matt. 28:18)

Jesus appeared to which of his followers after His resurrection?

Cleopas (Luke 24:13–35)

Mary and another woman (John 20:11–18, Luke 24:10)

Five hundred brethren (1 Cor. 15:6)

James (1 Cor. 15:7)

Eleven Disciples (John 20:19–29)

Apostles (John 21:1–14)

Paul (Acts 9:1–9)

What parallel elements are observed in Jesus' birth and death?

Two men named Joseph (father and Joseph of Arimathea, who
buried him) (John 6:42; John 19:38)

Myrrh (gift from the wise men and used to embalm body)
(Matt. 2:11, John 19:38–40)

Wrapped with cloth (swaddled as a baby and body wrapped for
burial) (Luke 2:7, Mark 15:42–47)

Borrowed rooms (stable and tomb) (Luke 2:7, Mark 15:42–47)

What negative names did Jesus use to describe people?

Hypocrites (Matt. 16:3)

Blind guides (Matt. 23:16)

Perverse generation (Matt. 17:17)

Fools (Matt. 23:17, 19)

Thieves (Matt. 21:13)

Generation of vipers (Matt. 23:33)

How is the term "Redeemer" referenced in the Bible?

My redeemer liveth (Job 19:25)

O Lord, my strength and redeemer (Ps. 19:14)

Their redeemer is mighty (Prov. 23:11)

Thy Redeemer, the mighty One of Jacob (Isa. 49:26)

The Redeemer shall come to Zion (Isa. 59:20)

Our Redeemer, Thy name is from everlasting (Isa. 63:16)

Thy redeemer, the Holy One of Israel (Isa. 41:14)

I the LORD am thy Saviour and thy Redeemer (Isa. 49:26)

Their Redeemer is strong (Jer. 50:34)

Fill in the blank: according to Matthew, the "Son of Man…"

… hath not where to lay His head (Matt. 8:20)

… hath power on earth to forgive sins (Matt. 9:6)

… is Lord even of the Sabbath day (Matt. 12:8)

… is He that soweth the good seed (Matt. 13:37)

… shall send forth His angels (Matt. 13:41)

… shall come in the glory of His Father with His angels (Matt. 16:27)

… will be raised again from the dead (Matt. 17:9)

… is come to save that which was lost (Matt. 18:11)

… shall be betrayed unto the chief priests and unto the scribes (Matt. 20:18)

… came not to be ministered unto, but to minister (Matt. 20:28)

What notable events mentioned in the Bible connect God or Jesus with the image of a tree?

> God warned Adam and Eve of the Tree of Knowledge of Good and
> Evil (Gen. 2:16–17)
>
> God sent cherubs to guard the Tree of Life (Gen. 3:22–24)
>
> The Lord appeared in Mamre and Isaac offered to rest under a tree
> (Gen. 18:1–4)
>
> Zechariah's vision of the Lord standing among myrtle trees
> (Zech. 1:8–11)
>
> Parable of the mustard seed grows into the greatest tree
> (Matt. 13:31–32)
>
> Jesus cursed the fruitless fig tree (Matt. 21:18–20)
>
> Jesus asked Zacchaeus to come down from a sycamore tree
> (Luke 19:1–5)
>
> Jesus saw Philip under a fig tree (John 1:45–48)
>
> Illustration of grafting a wild olive tree (Rom. 11:17)
>
> Saved people will eat from the Tree of Life amidst God's paradise
> (Rev. 2:7)

On what occasions was Mary Magdalene found at Jesus' feet?

> Sat at Jesus feet, listening, as Martha prepared food (Luke 10:39)
>
> When Lazarus died (John 11:32)
>
> Anoints Jesus' feet with ointment and wipes with her hair
> (John 12:3)
>
> At Golgotha during crucifixion (Mark 15:40)
>
> At the tomb where Jesus laid (Mark 15:47)
>
> When Jesus appeared to Mary after the resurrection (Mark 16:9)

Fill in the blank with statements pertaining to Jesus: "Verily, verily, I say unto you…"

The Son can do nothing of Himself, but what He seeth the Father do (John 5:19)

The hour is coming, and now is, when the dead shall hear the voice of the Son of God (John 5:25)

Ye seek me, not because ye saw the miracles, but because ye did eat of the loaves, and were filled (John 6:26)

Before Abraham was, I Am (John 8:58)

I am the door of the sheep (John 10:7)

The servant is not greater than his lord; neither He that is sent greater than He that sent Him (John 13:16)

He that receiveth whomsoever I send receiveth Me; and he that receiveth Me receiveth Him that sent Me (John 13:20)

That one of you shall betray Me (John 13:21)

The cock shall not crow, till thou hast denied Me thrice (John 13:38)

He that believeth on Me, the works that I do shall he do also (John 14:12)

According to Isaiah, Jesus shall be called what? Isaiah 9:6

Wonderful

Counselor

The mighty God

The everlasting Father

The Prince of Peace

When John asked, "Art thou he that should come," how did Jesus answer? Luke 7:22

The blind see

The deaf hear

The lame walk

The dead are raised

The lepers are cleansed

The Gospel is preached to the poor

How does Jesus counsel the rich young ruler? Mark 10:17–22

Do not commit adultery

Do not defraud

Do not murder

Honor your father and your mother

Do not steal

Sell whatever you have and give to the poor

Do not bear false witness

Take up the cross, and follow Me

What are the Fruits of the Spirit? Galatians 5:22–23

Love

Goodness

Joy

Faithfulness

Peace

Gentleness

Longsuffering

Self-Control

Kindness

What are sins against the Holy Spirit?

Blasphemy against the Holy Spirit (Matt. 12:31)

Defile the temple of the Holy Spirit (1 Cor. 3:16–17)

Speaketh against the Holy Spirit (Matt. 12:32)

Quench the Holy Spirit (1 Thess. 5:19)

Grieve the Holy Spirit (Eph. 4:30)

Despise the Holy Spirit (Heb. 10:26–29)

Lie to the Holy Spirit (Acts 5:1–11)

Fill in the blank regarding the Divine character: "Spirit of ..."

Spirit of God (Gen. 1:2)

Spirit of the living God (2 Cor. 3:3)

Spirit of the Lord (Judges 3:10)

Spirit of his Son (Gal. 4:6)

Spirit of your Father (Matt. 10:20)

Spirit of Jesus Christ (Phil. 1:19)

Spirit of holiness (Rom. 1:4)

Spirit of life in Christ Jesus (Rom. 8:2)

Spirit of life from God (Rev. 11:11)

Spirit of prophecy (Rev. 19:10)

What did God's spirit anoint Isaiah to do? Isaiah 61:1–3

Preach good tidings unto the meek

Proclaim the acceptable year of the Lord

Bind up the brokenhearted

Comfort all that mourn

Proclaim liberty to the captives

Appoint unto them that mourn in Zion

Open the prison to them that are bound

Give unto them beauty for ashes

What things should we not do to the Holy Spirit/Ghost?

Vex *(anger)* His Holy Spiri, (Isa. 63:10)

Blaspheme the Holy Ghost (Matt. 12:31)

Speaketh against the Holy Ghost, it shall not be forgiven him (Matt. 12:32)

Grieve not the Holy Spirit of God (Eph. 4:30)

Lie to the Holy Ghost (Acts 5:3)

Resist the Holy Ghost (Acts 7:51)

What are some things that provoked God to Anger? 2 Kings 17:16–17

Left all the commandments of the LORD

Made a molten image

Made a grove and worshipped and served Baal

Caused their sons and their daughters to pass through the fire

Used divination and enchantments

Sold themselves to do evil in the sight of the LORD

What ingredients of incense did God gave to Moses? Exodus 30:33–34 (NKJV)

Sweet spices

Galbanum

Stacte (gum resin)

Pure frankincense

Onycha

Seasoned with salt

Who did Christ give gifts to, in order to prepare holy people for the work of ministry? Ephesians 4:11, 12

Apostles

Prophets

Evangelists

Pastors

Teachers

Who were co-conspirators involved in the death of Jesus Christ?

Satan

Herod Antipas (Luke 23:11–12)

Judas Iscariot (Luke 22:48)

The Sanhedrin (Mark 14:55, NIV)

Caiaphas (John 11:49–53)

unnamed Roman centurion (Mark 15:39)

Pontius Pilate (Matt. 27:24)

Against whom did Jesus face trials/judgement?

Satan (Luke 4:2)

Pilate (John 18:28–38)

Annas (John 18:12–14, 19–23)

King Herod Antipas, (Luke 23:6–12)

Caiaphas (Matt. 26:57, 59–68)

Pilate (John 18:39; 19:6)

Sanhedrin (Luke 22:66–71, NKJV)

People reject the Messiah and pass judgement (John 19:7–16)

Things Numbered or Counted

How many good people in Sodom did Abraham mention in his bargain with God? Genesis 18:26–32

Fifty	Thirty
Forty-five	Twenty
Forty	Ten

What are "Important Threes" of the Bible?

Three wives of Noah's three sons (Gen. 7:13)

Three vine branches in butler's dream (Gen. 40:12)

Three baskets in the baker's dream (Gen. 40:18)

Three cities of safety (Deut. 19:9)

Three groups of Saul's soldiers to fight Ammonites (1 Sam. 11:11)

Three sons died the same day with their father Saul (1 Sam. 31:6)

Three feasts celebrated three times a year (2 Chron. 8:13)

Three daughters of Job (Job 1:4)

Three times a day, Daniel prays for three full weeks (Dan. 6:10)

Three Sabbath days, Paul discussed Scriptures with them (Acts 17:2)

What items in the Bible measure 3 cubits?
Moses' altar of burnt offering (Exod. 38:1)
Huram's ten bronze bases (stands) (1 Kings 7:27)
Solomon's bronze platform (2 Chron. 6:12–13)
Ezekiel's temple's porch (Ezek. 40:48)
Ezekiel's altar in his vision (Ezek. 41:22)

What were the six tribes of Israel with the largest populations?
Judah = 74,600 (Num. 1:27)
Dan = 62,700 (Num. 1:39)
Simeon = 59,300 (Num. 1:23)
Zebulun = 57,400 (Num. 1:31)
Issachar = 54,400 (Num. 1:29)
Naphtali = 53,400 (Num. 1:29)

What important groups of seven things are found in the Old Testament?
Seven pairs of unclean animals in Noah's Ark (Gen 7:2–4)
Seven ewe lambs to Abimelech for an oath for a well by Abraham
    (Gen. 21:28)
Seven cows and Seven ears of corn in Joseph's dreams (Gen. 41)
Seven sisters and one was Moses' wife (Exod. 2:16)
High Priest sprinkles blood on the altar Seven times (Lev. 4:6)
Seven candles in candlestick (Num. 8:2)
Seven times Naaman dipped in the Jordan River (2 Kings 5:10, 14)
Seven bullocks and Seven rams for Job's burnt offering (Job 42:8)
Job's Seven sons died and Seven sons born after troubles
    (Job 42:13)
The furnace was Seven times hotter for Daniel's friends (Dan 3:19)

What groups of seven things are found in Revelation?

Seven Churches (Rev. 1:4)

Seven Golden candlesticks (Rev. 1:12)

Seven Stars (Rev. 1:16)

Seven Spirits of God (Rev. 3:1)

Seven Lamps of fire burning (Rev. 4:5)

Seven Seals (Rev. 5:1)

Seven Horns (Rev. 5:6)

Seven Eyes (Rev. 5:6)

Seven Angels (Rev. 8:2)

Seven Trumpets (Rev. 8:2)

Seven Thunders (Rev. 10:3)

Seven Heads (Rev. 12:3)

Seven Crowns (Rev. 12:3)

Seven Golden Vials (Rev. 15:7)

Seven Mountains (Rev. 17:9)

Seven Kings (Rev. 17:10)

What things come in groups of seven in Pharoah's dream? Genesis 41

Fat and beautiful cows

Years of good crops and plenty to eat

Thin and ugly cows

Years of hunger

Full and good heads of grain

Stored food duing years of good crops

Thin and burned heads of grain

What amazing events of the Bible happen in seven days?

Seven days Creation (Gen. 1)

Seven days Noah was inside the Ark before it rained (Gen. 7:10)

Seven days before sending the dove the 2nd time (Gen. 8:10, 12)

Laban pursued Jacob for a seven days journey (Gen. 31:23)

Joseph mourned for his father seven days (Gen. 50:10)

Seven days shewbread was left on the table in the Temple and changed every Sabbath (Lev. 24:8)

Walls of Jericho fell after seven days (Joshua 6:4)

Samson's seven-day feast (Judges 14:12)

Samuel was late seven days (1 Sam.13:8)

Seven-day feast of Solomon for the Dedication of the Temple (2 Chron. 7:8–10)

What significant things in the Bible happen in seven years?

End of every Seven years thou shalt make a release (Deut. 15:1)

Seven years Jacob laboured for Leah (Gen. 29:18, 23)

Seven years Jacob labored Rachel (Gen. 29:20)

Seven years of abundance in Joseph's dreams (Gen. 41:29)

Seven years of famine in Joseph's dreams (Gen. 41:30)

David reigned seven years in Hebron (1 Kings 2:11)

Seven years of famine when woman's son was restored to life by Elisha (2 Kings 8:2)

Jehoash was Seven-years old when he began to reign (2 Kings 11:21)

King married Esther in seventh year of his reign (Esther 2:16)

Anna had been married only seven years (Luke 2:36)

What can ten shekels of silver or gold do in the Bible?

Abraham paid for the burial land (Gen. 23:15)

Isaac's servant gave Rebecca two bracelets of gold (Gen. 24:22)

Priest set a price for a promised woman (Lev. 27:5)

Micah paid ten shekels a year to a Levite (Judges 17:10)

Christ's parable of a woman having Ten pieces of silver (Luke 15:8)

What items come in groups of ten in relation to the temple?

Ten curtains of fine twined linen (Exod. 26:1)

Ten brass laver basins (1 Kings 7:27)

Ten commandments (Exod. 34:28)

Hiram made ten carts with bowls (1 Kings 7:40)

Ten post and bases (Exod. 38:12)

Ten candlesticks of gold (2 Chron. 4:7)

Ten bulls for offering (Num. 29:23)

Ten tables (2 Chron. 4:8)

Porch measured ten cubits width (1 Kings 6:3)

What groups of ten people are mentioned in the Bible?

Abraham bargained with God for ten good people (Gen. 18:32)

Joseph's ten brethren went to buy corn in Egypt (Gen. 42:3)

Haman's ten sons were hanged (Esther 9:14)

Gideon's ten servants destroyed Baal's altar (Judges 6:27)

Joab's ten armour bearers smote Absalom (2 Sam. 18:15)

Ten virgins at the wedding (Matt. 25:1)

Boaz took ten elders of the city as witnesses (Ruth 4:2)

Ten lepers that Jesus healed (Luke 17:12)

David's young men went to Nabal in Mt. Carmel (1 Sam. 25:5)

What things not relating to the temple come in groups of ten?

Abraham carries gifts on ten camels to Nahor (Gen. 24:10)

Laban changes Jacobs's wages ten times (Gen. 31:41)

David brought ten loaves and cheese to his brothers
    (1 Sam. 17:17–18)

Jeroboam's wife brought ten loaves to the prophet Ahijah to ask
    counsel (1 Kings 14:3)

Jehoahaz's ten chariots destroyed by king Aram (2 Kings 13:7)

The Lord brought the shadow ten degrees backward
    (2 Kings 20:9–11)

Daniel and his friends were found ten times better in wisdom and
    understanding (Dan. 1:20)

The ten horns and ten kings in Daniel's vision (Dan. 7:24)

The ten talents in Jesus' parable (Matt. 25:28)

What items come in groups of twelve that represent the twelve tribes in the Bible?

Twelve pillars of the altar (Exod. 24:4)

Twelve silver bowls (Num. 7:84)

Twelve silver chargers (Num. 7:84)

Twelve rods representing the children of Israel (Num. 17:2)

Twelve spoons of gold (Num. 7:84)

Twelve stones from the midst of the Jordan River (Joshua 4:3)

Ahijah rent the garment into twelve pieces (1 Kings 11:30)

Twelve baked cakes (Lev. 24:5)

Twelve thrones for the saints (Matt. 19:28)

Twelve cities comprise inheritance of each tribe (Joshua 19:15)

What groups of twelve things does John mention in Revelation?

A crown of twelve Stars (Rev. 12:1)

City had twelve foundations (Rev. 21:14)

High wall with twelve gates (Rev. 21:12)

Twelve angels at the gates (Rev. 21:12)

Names of the twelve tribes of Israel (Rev. 21:12)

Names of the twelve apostles of the lamb (Rev. 21:14)

Twelve pearl gates (Rev. 21:21)

Tree of life has twelve manners of fruit (Rev. 22:2)

Who was with groups of thirty unnamed people?

Jair—thirty sons (Judges 10:4)

Samson—with thirty men to Philistines (Judges 14:11–12)

Ibzan—thirty Sons and daughters (Judges 12:9)

Ibzan—thirty women he was not related to (Judges 12:9)

Samson—killed thirty Philistine men at Ashkelon (Judges 14:19)

Benjaminites—killed thirty Israelites soldiers (Judges 20:31)

Abdon—thirty nephews (Judges 12:14)

Samuel—invited thirty of Saul servants to eat (1 Sam. 9:22)

What is worth of thirty pieces of silver?
>   Payment for slave killed by bull (Exod. 21:32)
>   Priest's gave to Judas for Jesus (Matt. 26:15)
>   Judas gave back to the priest and leaders (Matt. 27:3)
>   Jeremiah's prophecy—"Israelites to pay for his life" (Matt. 27:9)
>   Price to buy the potter's field (Matt. 27:10)
>   They paid Zechariah thirty pieces of silver to cast unto the potter (Zech. 11:12, 13)

What groups of thirty are mentioned in the Bible?
>   Jacob—thirty camels for Esau (Gen. 32:15)
>   Jair's sons—thirty donkeys (Judges 10:4)
>   Samson—thirty linen shirts/clothes bet for a riddle (Judges 14:13)
>   Mithredath—took thirty gold bowls/dishes from the Lord's temple (Ezra 1:9)
>   Solomon—wrote thirty sayings of advice and wisdom (Prov. 22:20)
>   Ezekiel's vision—thirty rooms in the temple (Ezek. 41:6)
>   Zechariah—saw a flying scroll thirty feet long (Zech. 5:2, NIV)
>   Seed fell on good ground grew and produced thirty times more grain (Matt. 13:23)

What things measure thirty cubits?
>   Curtains used in the holy tabernacle (Exod. 26:8)
>   Huram melted bronze tank called "The Sea" (1 Kings 7:23)
>   Solomon built a house called "Forest of Lebanon" (1 Kings 7:2)
>   Solomon's temple Porch of Columns (1 Kings 7:6)
>   Solomon's temple (1 Kings 6:2)
>   Special kitchen in the temple's courtyard (Ezek. 46:22)

What things come in groups of forty?

Forty cows gift of Jacob to Esau (Gen. 32:15)

Forty silver bases for the temple tent (Exod. 36:24)

Forty ounces of silver fine for man who accused his wife
(Deut. 22:19, NIV)

Don't hit anyone more than forty times during punishment
(Deut. 25:3)

Abdon had forty sons (Judges 12:14)

Most holy place was forty cubits long (1 Kings 6:17)

Forty camels to carry Hazael's gift to Elisha (2 Kings 8:9)

Israelites stop times and camped in forty places (Num. 33:5–49)

Where is the number 120 used in the Bible?

Moses 120 years old when he died (Deut. 34:7)

Uriel led 120 people from the tribe of Kohath (1 Chron. 15:5)

There were 120 Levite singers with cymbals, lyres, and harps
(2 Chron. 5:12)

120 priests blew trumpets (2 Chron. 5:12)

There were 120 satraps under Daniel's supervision (Dan. 6:1)

There were 120 believers meeting with Peter (Acts 1:15)

Depth of the Adriatic Sea was 120 feet (Acts 27:28, NIV)

Where is the number 600 mentioned in the Bible?

Noah was 600 years old (Gen. 7:6)

Goliath's spear's head weighed 600 shekels of iron (1 Sam. 17:7)

Shamgar slew 600 Philistines (Judges 3:31)

600 men escaped with David from Saul (1 Sam. 23:13)

600 Danites, warriors from Zorah (Judges 18:11)

Solomon used six hundred shekels of gold for one target
(1 Kings 10:16)

600 men went with Samuel from Gilgal to Gibeah (1 Sam. 13:15)

600 shekels of silver per chariot (1 Kings 10:29)

600 men with Saul at Gibeah (1 Sam. 14:2)

David paid Ornan 600 shekels of gold for a threshing place
(1 Chron. 21:25)

For what projects did God give detailed measurements?

Noah's Ark (Gen. 6)

Courtyard of the Holy Tent (Exod. 27:9–19)

Ark of the Covenant (Exod. 25:10–22)

Altar for Burning Incense (Exod. 30:1–10)

Table (Exod. 25:23–30)

Holy Tent (Exod. 26)

Altar (Exod. 27:1–7)

Land distribution among the 12 tribes of Israel (Ezek. 47)

Ezekiel sees the Future Temple in Jerusalem (Ezek. 40)

The New Jerusalem that John saw (Rev. 21)

What groups of twelve people are mentioned in the Bible?

Ishmael's twelve princes (Gen. 17:20)

Jacob's twelve sons (Gen. 35:22)

Israel's twelve tribes (Gen. 49:28)

David's twelve men to fight with Ishbosheth (2 Sam. 2:15)

Ishbosheth's twelve men from the tribe of Benjamin (2 Sam. 2:15)

Solomon's twelve officers to provide provisions (1 Kings 4:7)

Twelve Chief Priests (Ezra 8:24)

Joshua's twelve spies (Joshua 4:4)

Jesus' twelve disciples (Matt. 10:1)

What things in the Bible measure ten cubits?

Acacia board's length for the holy tent (Exod. 26:16)

Temple's stone foundation (1 Kings 7:10)

Solomon's temple width (1 Kings 6:3)

Width of bronze bowl (1 Kings 7:23)

Cherubims of olive tree (1 Kings 6:23)

Holy Place temple door width (Ezek. 41:2)

What units of length and liquid measure are used in the Bible?

Cubit (Gen. 6:15)

Span (Exod. 28:16)

Hin (Exod. 29:40)

Homer (Lev. 27:16)

Pace (2 Sam. 6:13)

Finger (1 Kings 12:10)

Bath (1 Kings 7:26)

What units are used to measure weight and money in the Bible?

Shekel (Gen. 23:15)

Ephah (Exod. 16:36)

Talent (Exod. 25:39)

Gerah (Lev. 27:25)

Mina (1 Kings 10:17, NIV)

Farthing (Matt. 10:29)

Penny (Matt.20:2)

Mites (Mark 12:42)

Parables

Fill in the blank: "The kingdom of heaven is like…"

A grain of mustard seed (Matt. 13:31)

Unto leaven (Matt. 13:33)

Unto treasure hidden in a field (Matt. 13:44)

Unto a merchant man (Matt. 13:45)

Unto a net, that was cast into the sea (Matt. 13:47)

Unto a man that is a householder (Matt. 13:52)

A man who went out early in the morning to hire labourers (Matt. 20:1)

Unto a certain king, which made marriage for his son (Matt. 22:2)

What parables are about being faithful with God's gifts?

Good and bad fish (Matt. 13:47–52)

Wicked tenants (Matt. 21:33–44)

Talents or minas (Matt. 25:14–30)

Rich fool (Luke 12:13–21)

Dishonest steward (Luke 16:1–13)

What parables use illustrations related to plants or nature?

Sower and the seeds
(Matt. 13:3–9)
Growing seed (Mark 4:26–29)
Tares/Weeds (Matt. 13:24–30)
Patient husbandman
(Mark 4:26–29)
Mustard seed (Matt. 13:31)

Rich fool (Luke 12:16–21)
Wicked tenants
(Matt. 21:33–44)
Barren fig tree (Luke 13:6–9)
Budding fig tree (Matt. 24:32)
Grain of wheat (John 12:24)

What parables illustrate the Kingdom of Heaven?

Parable of the sower
(Matt. 13)
Pearl of great price (Matt. 13)
Tares (Matt. 13)
Laborers in the vineyard
(Matt. 21)
Mustard seed (Matt. 13)

Two sons (Matt. 21)
Leaven (Matt. 13)
Wicked husbandmen
(Matt. 21)
Hidden treasure (Matt. 13)
Great supper (Luke 14)

What parables of Jesus are found in three gospel books?

Great physician (Matt. 9:10–13, Mark 2:15–17, Luke 5:29–32)
Groom's attendants fasting (Matt. 9:14–15, Mark 2:18–20,
Luke 5:33–35)
New cloth and old cloth (Matt. 9:16, Mark 2:21, Luke 5:36)
New wine and old wineskin (Matt. 9:17, Mark 2:22, Luke 5:37–39)
Salt without taste (Matt. 5:13, Mark 9:50, Luke 14:34–35)
Ye are the light of the world (Matt. 5:14–16, Mark 4:21–23,
Luke 8:16–18)
Divided kingdom (Matt. 12:24–30, Mark 3:22–27, Luke 11:14–23)
Mustard seed (Matt. 13:31–32, Mark 4:30–32, Luke 13:18–19)
The Sower (4 types of soil) (Matt. 13:3–9, Mark 4:3–20,
Luke 8:4–15)
Landowner and wicked tenants (Matt. 21:33–46, Mark 12:1–12,
Luke 20:9–18)

Miracles

What miracles of Jesus Christ happened in nature?

Turning water into wine (John 2:1–3)

Walking on the water (Matt. 14:22–33)

Miraculous catch of fish (Luke 5:9)

Feeding the 4,000 (Mark 8:1–8)

Calming the storm (Mark 4:39)

Temple tax in the fish's mouth (Matt. 17:27)

Feeding the 5,000 (Matt. 14:13–21)

Withering of the fig tree (Mark 11:20–26)

What are the healing miracles of Jesus Christ?

    Epileptic boy (Matt. 17:14–16, NKJV)

    Man at Bethsaida (Mark 8:22)

    Cleansing of a leper/ten lepers (Matt. 8:2)

    Man with dropsy (Luke 14:2–4)

    Peter's mother-in-law (Matt. 8:14)

    Restoring a servant's ear (Luke 22:49–51)

    Man's withered hand/paralytic (Matt. 9:2)

    Infirm, bent woman (Luke 13:11)

    Hemorrhaging woman (Matt. 9:20)

    Nobleman's son (of fever) (John 4:46)

    Two blind men (Matt. 9:27)

    Man at Bethesda (John 5:1–18)

    Deaf mute (Mark 7:31–37)

What sickness did Jesus heal on the Sabbath Day?

    Withered hand in the Synagogue (Matt. 12:10–13)

    Simon's mother-in-law (Mark 1:30)

    Possessed with a devil, blind, and dumb (Matt. 12:22)

    Woman who had spirit infirmity (Luke 13:11)

    Man with dropsy (Luke 14:2)

    Man with unclean spirit/Possessed with devil (Mark 1:23)

    Invalid man (John 5:5, NIV)

At what times did Jesus heal the blind?

    Two blind men (Matt. 9:27–31)

    Blind man at Bethsaida (Mark 8:22–26)

    Man born blind (John 9:1–12)

    Blind, mute demoniac (Matt. 12:22–23)

    Restores sight to Bartimaeus (Mark 10:46–52)

At what times did Jesus heal by casting out demons?

Demoniac in synagogue at Capernaum (Luke 4:31–37)

Two demoniacs at a tomb near Gadara; devils cast out to swine (Matt. 8:28–34)

Mute man oppressed by a demon; after demons cast out, man spoke (Matt. 9:32–34)

Gentile woman with a demoniac daughter in the region of Tyre and Sidon (Matt. 15:21–28)

Epileptic boy possessed of the devil (Matt. 17:14–21)

Blind, deaf demoniac was able to speak and see (Matt. 12:22)

What amazing things did Jesus do in Capernaum?

Healed a paralyzed man (Matt. 9:2)

Called Matthew as a disciple (Matt. 9:9)

Healed a servant of the Roman centurion (Matt. 8:5)

Healed the daughter of Jairus (Luke 8:41–42)

Jesus taught about the bread of life (John 6:35)

Jesus paid the temple tax with money from a fish (Matt. 17:24–27)

What things did Jesus do in Galilee?

Healed the leper (Mark 1:39–41)

Sent out the 12 apostles to preach (Matt. 10:5)

Healed a man with shriveled hand (Mark 3:1)

Walked on the water (John 6:19)

Calmed a storm (Matt. 8:24)

Made a prophecy of his last days (Matt. 17:22–23)

What healing miracles of Jesus are recorded in three Gospels books?

Heals Peter's mother-in-law (Matt. 8:16–17; Mark 1:29–31; Luke 4:38–39)

Cleanses a man with leprosy (Matt. 8:1–4; Mark 1:40–45; Luke 5:12–14)

Heals a paralytic (Matt. 9:1–8; Mark 2:1–12; Luke 5:17–26)

Heals a man's withered hand (Matt. 12:9–14; Mark 3:1–6; Luke 6:6–11)

Casts demons into a herd of pigs (Matt. 8:28–33; Mark 5:1–20; Luke 8:26–39)

Heals a bleeding woman in the crowd (Matt. 9:20–22; Mark 5:25–34; Luke 8:42–48)

Raises Jairus' daughter to life (Matt. 9:18; Mark 5:21–24; Luke 8:40–42)

Heals an epileptic boy with a demon (Matt. 17:14–20; Mark 9:14–29; Luke 9:37–43)

Restores sight to Bartimaeus (Matt. 20:29–34; Mark 10:46–52; Luke 18:35–43)

What "Mysteries" are spoken of in the Bible?

Mysteries of the kingdom of heaven (Matt. 13:11)

Mystery of the gospel (Eph. 6:19)

Speak the wisdom of God in a mystery (1 Cor. 2:7)

Mystery of iniquity (2 Thes. 2:7)

Speak the mystery of Christ (Col. 4:3)

Mystery of the faith in a pure conscience (1 Tim. 3:9)

Mystery of His will (Eph. 1:9)

Mystery of godliness (1 Tim. 3:16)

Mystery of the husband and wife and the church (Eph. 5:31–39)

Mystery of the seven stars (Rev. 1:20)

What miracles are associated with Elijah?

    Causing the rain to cease for 3 1/2 years (1 Kings 17:1)
    Being fed by the ravens (1 Kings 17:4)
    Miracle of the barrel of meal and cruse of oil (1 Kings 17:14)
    Resurrection of the widow's son (1 Kings 17:22)
    Calling of fire from heaven on the altar (1 Kings 18:38)
    Causing it to rain (1 Kings 18:45)
    Calling fire from heaven upon the first and second sets of
       50 soldiers (2 Kings 1:10, 2 Kings 1:12)
    Parting of the Jordan (2 Kings 2:8)
    Being caught up to heaven in a whirlwind (2 Kings 2:11)

What miracles are associated with Elisha?

    Parting and crossing the Jordan (2 Kings 2:14)
    Filling of the valley with water (2 Kings 3:17)
    Miracle of the vessels of oil (2 Kings 4:4)
    Resurrection of the Shunammite's son (2 Kings 4:34)
    Miracle of the bread (2 Kings 4:43)
    Perception of Gehazi's transgression (2 Kings 5:26)
    Floating of the axe head (2 Kings 6:6)
    Giving vision of the chariots to the young man (2 Kings 6:17)
    Deception of the Moabites with the valley of blood (2 Kings 3:22)
    Deception of the Syrians with the sound of chariots (2 Kings 7:6)

What healing and/or cursing miracles happened in the career of Elisha?

    Healing the waters of Jericho (2 Kings 2:21)
    Cursing Gehazi with leprosy (2 Kings 5:27)
    Curse of the she bears to maul a group of children for making fun
       of a man for being bald (2 Kings 2:24)
    Restoring the sight of the Syrian army (2 Kings 6:20)
    Smiting the Syrian army with blindness, 2 Kings 6:18
    Healing of the gourds (2 Kings 4:41)
    Resurrection of the man touched by his bones (2 Kings 13:21)
    Healing of Naaman (2 Kings 5:14)

What are the miracles of Peter?

    Healed the cripple at Gate Beautiful (Acts 3:11)

    Peter's shadow caused healing (Acts 5:15)

    Aeneas healed from palsy (Acts 9:33, 34)

    Dorcas raised from dead (Acts 9:40)

    Deliverance from prison (Acts 12:7)

What are the miracles of Paul?

    Eutychus raised after falling out of window (Acts 20:8–10)

    Healed a possessed girl at Phillipi (Acts 16:16–19)

    Healed a crippled man at Lystra (Acts 14:8–11)

    Elymas, the sorcerer, blinded by Paul (Acts 13:8–14)

    Healed the governor of Malta (Acts 28:7–9)

    Believers at Ephesus spoke in tongues (Acts 19:1–6)

    Bitten by a snake but did not die (Acts 28:3–6)

What special or miraculous events happened in Jordan River?

    Jesus baptised in Jordan River (Matt. 3:13)

    Israel crossed the Jordon while Joshua led them (Joshua 3)

    Naaman, captain of the host of the king of Syria, dipped seven times in the Jordan to heal his leprosy (2 Kings 5:14)

    Elijah smote the water then Elisha and Elijah walk on dry ground (2 Kings 2:8)

    Elisha smote the water and the Jordan splits and he walks across (2 Kings 2:14)

    Elisha floats the axe head in the Jordan (2 Kings 6:1–7)

What healing miracles were performed by the Disciples?

Lame man at the Gate Beautiful by Peter and John (Acts 3:1–16)

Sick in the streets by Peter and other disciples (Acts 5:15)

Stephen's great wonders and miracles (Acts 6:8)

Healing miracles at Samaria by Philip (Acts 8:5–8)

Aeneas, who had been bedridden eight years and was paralyzed, healed by Peter (Acts 9:33–34)

Raising Dorcas from the dead by Peter (Acts 9:36)

Brother Ananias lays hands on Saul of Tarsus to restore his sight (Acts 9:17–18)

Crippled man at Lystra healed by Paul (Acts 14:8–10)

Paul restores life to Eutychus (Acts 20:9–12)

Healing of Publius' father by Paul (Acts 28:7–8)

Prophecies

What are the prophecies of Elijah?
Ahab's sons would all be destroyed (1 Kings 21:22)
Jezebel would be eaten by dogs (1 Kings 21:23)
Ahaziah would die of his illness (2 Kings 1:4)
Elisha would have a double portion of his spirit (2 Kings 2:10)

What are the prophecies of Elisha?
Shunammite woman would have a son (2 Kings 4:16)
Syrian battle plans (2 Kings 6:9)
End of the great famine (2 Kings 7:1)
Scoffing nobleman would see, but not partake of, the abundance
(2 Kings 7:2)
Seven-year famine (2 Kings 8:1)
Benhadad's untimely death (2 Kings 8:10)
Hazael's cruelty to Israel (2 Kings 8:12)
Jehu would smite the house of Ahab (2 Kings 9:7)
Joash would smite the Syrians at Aphek (2 Kings 13:17)
Joash would smite Syria thrice but not consume it (2 Kings 13:19)

What are the elements of the description of the "Man" in Daniel's vision?
Daniel 10:5, 6

Clothed in linen
Eyes as lamps of fire
Loins were girded with fine gold of Uphaz
Arms and his feet like in colour to polished brass
Body also was like the beryl
Voice of his words like the voice of a multitude
Face as the appearance of lightning

What were Zechariah's visions?
A man among the myrtle trees (Zech. 1:7–17)
Four horns and the four craftsmen (Zech. 1:18–21)
Surveyor with a measuring line (Zech. 2:1–12)
Cleansing and crowning of Joshua, the High Priest (Zech. 3)
Gold lampstand and the two olive trees (Zech. 4)
Flying scroll (Zech. 5:1–4)
Woman in a basket (Zech. 5:5–11)
Four chariots (Zech. 6:1–8)

What are the prophecies concerning the Messiah, excluding prophecies of his birth and death?
Taken to Egypt (Hosea 11:1; Matt. 2:14–15)
Anointed by the Holy Spirit (Isa. 11:2; Matt. 3:16–17)
Would perform miracles (Isa. 35:5–6; Matt. 9:35)
Would minister in Galilee/preach good news (Isa. 9:1; Matt. 4:12–16)
Would cleanse the Temple (Mal. 3:1; Matt. 21:12–13)
Would first present Himself as King (Dan. 9:25; Matt. 21:4–11)
Would enter Jerusalem as a king on a donkey (Zech. 9:9; Matt. 21:4–9)
Would be rejected by the Jews (Ps. 118:22; 1 Pet. 2:7)
Would rise from the dead (Ps. 16:10; Mark 16:6)
Would ascend into Heaven and sit at the right hand of God
   (Ps. 68:18; Heb. 1:3)

What prophecies concern the End of the Age?

An increase in disasters and wars (Matt. 24:3–7)

Rise in false religious leaders and those claiming to be Christ (Matt. 24:4–5)

A falling away from the true faith in Jesus Christ (Matt. 24:10)

Knowledge and travel will be greatly increased (Dan. 12:4)

Increase in wickedness and a decrease in morals (Matt. 24:12, 37)

Attitudes of men in the last days (2 Tim. 3:1–5)

The emergence of a world leader (Rev. 13:3–8)

The mark of the beast (Rev. 13:16, 17)

What are Zechariah's prophecies of Jerusalem? Zechariah 14:1–5

The Day of the Lord is coming

Nations will gather to fight against Jerusalem

The City will be captured

Houses ransacked and possessions will be plundered and divided up

Women raped

Half of the city will go into exile

The rest of the people will not be taken from the city

The Lord will go out and fight against those nations

The Mount of Olives will be split in two from east to west, forming a great valley

People will flee by the mountain valley

What is the description of the 4th beast in Daniel's vision? Daniel 7:3, 7, 8

Came up from the sea

Had ten horns

Dreadful and terrible, and exceedingly strong

There came up among them another little horn

Had great iron teeth

Three of the first horns plucked up by the roots

Stamped the residue with the feet of it

This [little] horn had eyes like the eyes of man

Diverse from all the beasts that were before it

Mouth speaking great things

What visions are found in both Daniel and Revelation?

The worship of the beast's statue (Dan. 3:5–7, 15; Rev. 13:15)

The leopard, the bear, and the lion (Dan. 7:4–6; Rev. 13:2)

The beast boasting and mouthing blasphemies (Dan. 7:8, 11; Rev. 13:5)

The Son of Man coming on the glory-cloud (Dan. 7:13; Rev. 1:7)

The war against the saints (Dan. 7:21; Rev. 13:7)

The ten horns (Dan. 7:8; Rev. 12:3; 13:1)

A three-and-a-half time period (Dan. 12:7; Rev. 11:9, 11)

What characteristics does John describe in his vision of the beast rising up from the sea? Revelation 13:1–6

Having seven heads and ten horns

Upon his horns were ten crowns

Upon his heads the name of blasphemy

Like unto a leopard

His feet were as the feet of a bear

His mouth as the mouth of a lion

Dragon gave him his power, his seat, and great authority

One of his heads was wounded to the death

His deadly wound was healed and all the world wondered after the beast.

Worshipped the dragon which gave power unto the beast

Describe what John saw in his vision about the Angel and the Little Scroll? Revelation. 10:1–7

Clothed with a cloud

A rainbow was upon his head

His face was as it were the sun

His feet as pillars of fire

He had in his hand an open little book

He set his right foot upon the sea, and his left foot on the earth

Cried with a loud voice, as when a lion roareth

Seven thunders uttered their voices

The angel lifted up his hand to heaven to sware by him that leveth forever and ever.

What people and body parts are used as symbols in Bible prophecy and what do they represent?

Woman = True/Apostate Church (Eph. 5:23–27)

Harlot = Apostate Church (Jer. 3:6–9)

Thief = Suddenness of Jesus' coming (2 Pet. 3:10)

Heads = Major powers/Rulers/Governments (Rev. 17:9)

Forehead = Mind (Ezek. 3:8)

Eyes = Spiritual Discernment (Matt. 13:10–17)

Skin = Christ's righteousness (1 Pet. 1:19)

Hand = Deeds/Works/Actions (Isa. 59:6)

Feet = Directions (Ps.119:105)

What are the signs of the End Time from nature, the Word, in the Church?

Earthquakes (Luke 21:11)

Increase in crimes (2 Tim. 3:1)

Pestilence and disease (Matt. 24:7)

Famine (Matt. 24:7)

Hail (Job 38:22–23)

Persecution (Matt. 24:9–10)

Wars and conflicts (Matt. 24:6)

What celestial signs appear after opening the sixth seal? Revelation 6:12–17

Great earthquake

Stars fell

Sun turned black

Sky was rolled back as a scroll

Moon turned blood-red

Earth's population was terrified

How does John describe the "Son of Man" seen in his vision?
Revelation 1:9–17

Clothed with garment to foot

Feet like fine brass as if burned in furnace

Girded with golden girdle

Voice as the sound of many waters

Head and hair were like wool

Had seven stars in His right hand

Head and hair were white as snow

Mouth is like a sharp, two-edged sword

Eyes were as flame of fire

Countenance (face) is as the sun shineth

Kings and Prophets

Who were the first ten Kings of Judah? *(Southern Kingdom)*

Rehoboam (1 Kings 14:21–31)   Jehoram (2 Kings 8:16–24)

Abijam (1 Kings 15:1–8)   Joash (2 Chron. 24:1–27)

Asa (1 Kings 15:9–24)   Amaziah (2 Chron. 25:1–28)

Jehoshaphat (1 Kings 22:41–50)   Uzziah (2 Chron. 26:1–23)

Ahaziah (2 Kings 8:25–9:29)   Jotham (2 Chron. 27:1–9)

Who were the first ten Kings of Israel? *(Northern Kingdom)*

Jeroboam (1 Kings 11:26–40)   Omri (1 Kings 16:21–28)

Baasha (1 Kings 15:16–22)   Ahab (1 Kings 16:29–22)

Nadab (1 Kings 15:25–31)   Ahaziah (1 Kings 22:51–53)

Elah (1 Kings 16:8–14)   Joram (2 Kings 3:1–9:26)

Zimri (1 Kings 16:15–20)   Jehu (2 Kings 9:1–10:36)

Who were the first ten Prophets of Judah? *(Southern Kingdom)*
Shemaiah (2 Chron. 11:2–4)
Iddo the Seer (2 Chron. 12:15)
Azariah (2 Chron. 15:1)
Hanani (2 Chron. 16:7–10)
Jehu, son of Hanani (2 Chron. 19:2, 3)
Jahaziel (2 Chron. 20:14–17)
Eliezer (2 Chron. 20:37)
Elijah (2 Chron. 21:12–15)
Obadiah
Joel

Who were the first ten Prophets of Israel? *(Northern Kingdom)*
Ahijah the Shilonite (1 Kings 11:29–39)
Jehu, son of Hanani (1 Kings 16:1–7)
Elijah (1 Kings 17–21)
Elisha (1 Kings 19:19–21)
Micaiah, son of Imlah (1 Kings 22:8–28)
Iddo the Seer (2 Chron. 9:29)
Obed the Prophet (2 Chron. 28:9–11)
Jonah
Amos
Hosea

What kings are buried in the city of David?
David (1 Kings 2:10)
Solomon (1 Kings 11:43)
Rehoboam (1 Kings 14:31)
Abijam (1 Kings 15:8)
Asa (1 Kings 15:24)
Jehoshaphat (1 Kings 22:50)
Joram (2 Kings 8:24)
Azariah (2 Kings 15:7)
Jotham (2 Kings 15:38)
Ahaz (2 Kings 16:20)

Who were the kings of Judah while Israel was exiled or in captivity?
Hezekiah (2 Kings 18:1)
Manasseh (2 Kings 21:1)
Amon (2 Kings 21:19)
Josiah (2 Kings 22:1)
Jehoahaz (2 Kings 23:31)
Jehoiakim (2 Kings 23:36)
Jehoiachin (2 Kings 24:8)
Zedekiah (2 Kings 24:18)

What kings "slept with his fathers" and were buried in Samaria?
Omri (1 Kings 16:28)
Jehu (2 Kings 10:35)
Jehoahaz (2 Kings 13:9)
Joash (2 Kings 13:13)
Jehoash (2 Kings 14:16)

What kings "slept with his fathers" and were buried in other places?
Baasha—in Tirzah (1 Kings 16:6)
Manasseh—in the garden in Uzza (2 Kings 21:18)
Uzziah—with his fathers in the field (2 Chron. 26:23)
Ahaz—in Jerusalem (2 Chron. 28:27)
Hezekiah—in the chiefest sepulchres (2 Chron. 32:33)

What king "slept with his fathers" and whose burial place was not mentioned?
Jeroboam—father of Nadab (1 Kings 14:20)
Ahab (1 Kings 22:20)
Menahem (2 Kings 15:22)
Hezekiah (2 Kings 20:21)
Jeroboam, father of Zachariah (2 Kings 14:29)
Jehoiakim (2 Kings 24:6)

The acts of what kings are written in the book of the chronicles of the Kings of Israel?

Jeroboam (1 Kings 14:19)

Zachariah (2 Kings 15:11)

Shallum (2 Kings 15:15)

Pekahiah (2 Kings 15:26)

Pekah (2 Kings 15:31)

The acts of which of Israel's kings is not written in the book of the chronicles of the kings?

Nadab (1 Kings 15:31)

Ahab (1 Kings 22:39)

Baasha (1 Kings 16:5)

Elah (1 Kings 16:14)

Zimri (1 Kings 16:20)

Omri (1 Kings 22:27)

Jehu (2 Kings 10:34)

Ahaziah (2 Kings 1:18)

Jehoahaz (2 Kings 13:8)

Jehoash (2 Kings 14:15)

The acts of what kings are not written in the book of the chronicles of the kings of Judah?

Rehoboam (1 Kings 1:29)

Abijam (1 Kings 15:7)

Asa (1 Kings 15:23)

Jehoshaphat (1 Kings 22:45)

Joash (2 Kings 12:19)

Amaziah (2 Kings 14:18)

Azariah (2 Kings 15:6)

Jotham (2 Kings 15:36)

Joram (2 Kings 8:23)

Ahaz (2 Kings 16:19)

Which kings of Israel or Judah reigned one year or less?

Zimri—Israel—seven days (1 Kings 16:10)

Jehoiachin—Judah—three months (2 Chron. 36:9)

Shallum—Israel—one month (2 Kings 15:10)

Zachariah—Israel—six months (2 Kings 14:29)

Jehoahaz—Judah—three months (2 Kings 23:30–31)

Ahaziah—Judah—one year (2 Chron. 22:1–2)

What kings of Judah were recorded as "good"? *(part of reign good)*

David (Hosea 3:5)

Solomon (1 Chron. 29:28)

Asa (2 Chron.14:2)

Jehoshapat (1 Kings 22:42–43)

Joash (Judges 8:32)

Amaziah (2 Chron. 25:1–2)

Uzziah or Azariah (Isa. 6:1)

Jotham (2 Kings 15:32–34)

Hezekiah (2 Chron. 32:32)

Josiah (2 Chron. 35:26)

What kings of Judah reigned for more than fifteen years?

Manasseh—fifty-five years (2 Chron. 33:1)

Jehoshaphat—twenty-five years (2 Chron. 20:31)

Azariah (Uzziah)—fifty-two years (Chron. 26:3)

Rehoboam—seventeen years (1 Kings 14:21)

Asa—forty-one years (1 Kings 15:9–10)

Jotham—sixteen years (2 Chron. 27:1)

Joash—forty years (2 Chron. 24:1)

Ahaz—sixteen years (2 Kings 16:2)

Josiah—thirty-one years (2 Kings 22:1)

Amaziah—twenty-nine years (2 Kings 14:1–2)

Hezekiah—twenty-nine years (2 Chron. 29:1)

What kings of Israel reigned for more than fifteen years?

Jeroboam II—forty-one years (2 Kings 14:23)

Jehoahaz—seventeen years (2 Kings 13:1)

Jehu—twenty-eight years (2 Kings 9:13)

Jehoash—sixteen years (2 Kings 13:9)

Baasha—twenty-four years (1 Kings 15:33)

Jeroboam 1—twenty-two years (1 Kings 12:20)

Ahab—twenty-two years (1 Kings 16:29)

Pekah—twenty years (2 Kings 15:27)

What kings of Judah died of old age?

David (1 Chron. 29:28)

Solomon (2 Chron. 9:31)

Rehoboam (2 Chron. 12:16)

Abijah (2 Chron. 14:1)

Jehoshaphat (2 Chron. 21:1)

Jotham (2 Chron. 27:9)

Ahaz (2 Chron. 28:27)

Hezekiah (2 Chron. 32:33)

Manasseh (2 Chron. 33:20)

Jehoiakim (2 Kings 24:6)

What kings of Israel died of old age?

David (1 Chron. 29:28)

Solomon (2 Chron. 9:31)

Jeroboam I (1 Kings 14:20)

Baasha (1 Kings 16:6)

Omri (1 Kings 16:28)

Jehu (2 Kings 10:35

Jehoahaz (2 Kings 13:9)

Jehoash/Joash (2 Kings 13:13)

Jeroboam II (2 Kings 14:29)

Menahem (2 Kings 15:22)

What kings of Israel were sons of his predecessor?

Nadab (1 Kings 14:20)

Elah (1 Kings 16:6)

Ahab (1 Kings 16:28)

Ahaziah (1 Kings 22:40)

Jehoram (Joram), 1 Kings 22:50

Jehoahaz (2 Kings 10:35)

Jehoash/Joash (2 Kings 13:9)

Jeroboam II (2 Kings 14:16)

Zachariah (2 Kings 14:29)

Pekahiah (2 Kings 15:22)

What kings of Judah were sons of his predecessor?

Rehoboam (1 Kings 12:21–23)

Abijam (1 Kings 14:31)

Asa (1 Kings 15:8)

Jehoshaphat (1 Kings 15:24)

Jehoram (1 Kings 22:50)

Ahaziah (2 Kings 8:24)

Amaziah (2 Kings 12:21)

Azariah (Uzziah)
   (2 Kings 14:16–17)

Jotham (2 Kings 15:7)

Ahaz (2 Kings 15:38)

Hezekiah (2 Kings 16:20)

Manasseh (2 Kings 20:21)

Amon (2 Chron. 33:20)

Josiah (2 Kings 21:25–26)

Jehoahaz (2 Kings 23:30)

Jehoiakim (1 Chron. 3:15)

Jehoiachin (2 Kings 24:6)

Zedekiah (2 Chron. 36:10)

What kings of Israel were murdered by his successor?

Nadab by Baasha (1 Kings 15:25–28)

Elah by Zimri (1 Kings 16:9–10)

Jehoram by Jehu (2 Kings 9:24–25)

Zachariah by Shallum (2 Kings 15:10)

Shallum by Menahem (2 Kings 15:14)

Pekahiah by Pekah (2 Kings 15:25)

Pekah by Hosea (2 Kings 15:30)

What kings or queens of Judah were murdered?

Ahaziah by Jehu (2 Kings 9:27)

Athaliah by army assigned by Jehoiada (2 Chron. 23:14–15)

Joash/(Jehoash) by his officials (2 Kings 12:20–21)

Amaziah by men sent by his officials (2 Chron. 25:27)

Amon by his officials (2 Kings 21:23)

Josiah shot by Neco's archers (2 Chron. 35:23–24)

What kings of Judah "had done evil in the sight of the Lord?"

Solomon (1 Kings 11:6)

Jehoahaz (2 Kings 23:32)

Jehoram (2 Kings 3:1–2)

Jehoiakim (2 Kings 23:37)

Ahaziah, son of Jehoram (2 Kings 8:27)

Jehoiachin (2 Kings 24:9)

Manasseh (2 Kings 21:2)

Zedekiah (2 Kings 24:19)

Amon (2 Kings 21:20)

What kings of Israel "had done evil in the sight of the Lord?"

Jeroboam (2 Kings 14:24)

Ahaziah, son of Ahab (1 Kings 22:52)

Nadab (1 Kings 15:25–27)

Jehoahaz (2 Kings 13:2)

Baasha (1 Kings 15:33–34)

Jehoash (2 Kings 13:11)

Zimri (1 Kings 16:18–19)

Zechariah (2 Kings 15:9)

Ahab (1 Kings 16:30)

Menahem (2 Kings 15:18)

What kings or queens of Judah are not a child of the forerunner?
(previous king)

Athaliah—Mother (2 Kings 11:1–20)
Joash—Grandson (2 Kings 11:1–12:2)
Jehoiakim—Brother (2 Chron. 36:4–8)
Zedekiah—Uncle (2 Kings 24:17–25:30)

What kings of Israel are not a child of the forerunner? (previous king)
Baasha—none (1 Kings 15:25–28)
Zimri—Captain of Chariots (1 Kings 16:9–10)
Omri—Army Captain (1 Kings 16:16–28)
Joram—Brother (2 Kings 9:14–24)
Jehu (2 Kings 9–10)
Shallum (2 Kings 15:10–15)
Menahem (2 Kings 15:14–22)
Pekah—Army Captain (2 Kings 15:25–38)
Hoshea (2 Kings 17:1–6)

What kings were conquered by Joshua and the children of Israel?
Joshua 12:8–24

King of Jericho
Japhia, king of Lachish
King of Ai, beside Bethel
Debir, king of Eglon
Adonizedek, king of Jerusalem
Horam, king of Gezer
Hoham, king of Hebron
King of Debir
Piram, king of Jarmuth
King of Geder
King of Hormah
King of Bethel
King of Arad
King of Tappuah

King of Libnah
King of Hepher
King of Adullam
King of Aphek
King of Lasharon
King of Madon
King of Megiddo
King of Hazor
King of Kedesh
King of Shimron Meron
King of Jokneam in Carmel
King of Akshaph
King of Dor
King of Taanach
King of Goyim in Gilgal

The Bible uses the term, "And the Lord said unto" regarding which kings?

David (1 Sam. 23:2)

Solomon (1 Kings 9:3)

Sedekiah (1 Kings 22:22)

Ahab (2 Chron. 18:20)

What five kings hid in a cave while Joshua made war when the sun stood still? Joshua 10:1–27

Adonizedec, king of Jerusalem

Hoham, king of Hebron

Piram, king of Jarmuth

Japhia, king of Lachish

Debir, king of Eglon

What Levites were sent by Jehoshaphat to teach Judah the Law of the Lord? 2 Chronicles 17:7–8

Shemaiah	Tobijah
Jehonathan	Asahel
Nethaniah	Tobadonijah
Adonijah	Shemiramoth
Zebadiah	

What princes and priests were sent by Jehoshaphat to teach Judah the Law of the Lord? 2 Chronicles 17:7–8

Benhail

Michaiah

Obadiah

Elishama

Zechariah

Jehoram

Nethaneel

Who are the kings and princes of Persia mentioned in the Bible?
Cyrus (Ezra 1–3)
Artaxerxes (Ezra 4:7–23)
Darius (Ezra 5:6)
Ahasureus (KJV) Xerxes (NIV) (Ezra 4:6)
Carshena (Esther 1:14)
Shethar (Esther 1:14)
Admatha (Esther 1:14)
Tarshish (Esther 1:14)
Meres (Esther 1:14)
Marsena (Esther 1:14)
Memucan (Esther 1:14)

What king died by hanging on a tree?
King of Ai (Joshua 8:29)
Debir, king of Eglon (Joshua 10:23, 26)
Adonizedec king of Jerusalem (Joshua 10:23, 26)
Saul, king of Israel (2 Sam. 21:12–13)
Hoham, king of Hebron (Joshua 10:23, 26)
Absalom (2 Sam. 18:10)
Piram, king of Jarmuth (Joshua 10:23, 26)
Jesus (Acts 5:30)
Japhia, king of Lachish (Joshua 10:23, 26)

What kings were buried in Samaria?
Omri (1 Kings 16:28)
Jehoahaz (2 Kings 13:9)
Ahab (1 Kings 22:37)
Joash (2 Kings 13:13)
Jehu (2 Kings 10:35)
Jehoash (2 Kings 14:16)

What five Amorite kings allied together to fight Gideon? Joshua 10:23, 26

Adonizedec, king of Jerusalem

Hoham, king of Hebron

Piram, king of Jarmuth

Japhia, king of Lachish

Debir, king of Eglon

What are the names of the kings of Babylon?

Berodach-baladan (2 Kings 20:12)

Nebuchadnezzar (2 Kings 24:1)

Artaxerxes (Neh. 13:6)

Evil-merodach (Jer. 52:31)

Belshazzar (Dan. 7:1)

What kings did Moses defeat on the way to Canaan?

Pharaoh (Exod. 15:4, 5)

Evi of Midian (Num. 31:7–12)

Amalek (Exod. 17:8–18)

Rekem of Midian (Num. 31:7–12)

King of Arad, the Canaanite (Num. 21:1–3)

Zur of Midian (Num. 31:7–12)

Sihon of the Amorites (Num. 21:21–24)

Hur of Midian (Num. 31:7–12)

Og of Bashan (Num. 21:33–35)

Reba of Midian (Num. 31:7–12)

Who were the Edomites dukes who came from Esau? Genesis 36:40–43

Duke Timnah	Duke Aholibamah
Duke Pinon	Duke Mibzar
Duke Alvah	Duke Elah
Duke Kenaz	Duke Magdiel
Duke Jetheth	Duke Iram
Duke Teman	

Who issued decrees in the Bible?

King Hezekiah and his assembly (2 Chron. 30:1–5)

Queen Esther (Esther 9:32)

King Cyrus of Babylon (Ezra 5:13)

Nebuchadnezzar (Dan. 2:15)

King Darius (Ezra 6:1)

King of Nineveh (Jonah 3:6–7)

King Artaxerxes of Persia (Ezra 7:21)

Caesar Augustus (Luke 2:1)

King Ahasuerus (Esther 2:1)

King Herod (Matt. 2:16)

What kings or priests were married, but his wife was not named in the Bible?

Abimelech, king of Philistines (Gen. 20:17)

King Belshazzar (Dan. 5:2)

King Solomon (1 Kings 11:3–4)

Amaziah king of Judah (Amos, 7:14–17)

King Jeroboam (1 Kings 14:2)

Eleazar the priest (Ex. 6:25)

Jehoiachin, king of Judah (2 Kings 24:15)

Eli the priest (1 Sam. 2:12)

King Jehoram (2 Chron. 21:5–6)

Jehoiada the priest (2 Chron. 24:3)

Who were queens or wives of kings?

Sheba (1 Kings 10:1)	Vashti (Esther 1:9)
Jezebel (1 Kings 21)	Bathsheba (2 Sam. 11)
Tahpenes (1 Kings 11:19)	Esther (Esther 5:2)
Michaiah (2 Kings 22)	Michal (1 Sam. 18:20–28)
Maachah (1 Kings 15:13)	Candace (Acts 8:27)
Abihail (1 Sam. 25)	Ahinoam (1 Sam. 14:50)

Who were the wives of King David?
   Michal, daughter of Saul (1 Sam. 18:26)
   Ahinoam, the Jezreelitess (1 Chron. 3:1)
   Abigail, the Carmelitess (1 Sam 25:3)
   Maachah, daughter of Talmai (2 Sam. 3:3)
   Haggith (1 Chron. 3:1–5)
   Abital (2 Sam. 3:4)
   Eglah (2 Sam. 3:5)
   Bathsheba (2 Sam. 2:24)
   Abishag (1 Kings 1:15)

Who were the wives of the kings of Judah?
   Mahalath/Maachah = King Rehoboam (2 Chron. 11:18)
   Azubah = King Asa (1 Kings 22:42, 1 Kings 15:24)
   Jehoaddan = King Joash (2 Kings 14:1, 2)
   Jecholiah = King Amaziah (2 Kings 15:2)
   Jerusha = King Uzziah (2 Kings 15:32, 33)
   Zibiah = King Ahaziah (2 Kings 12:1)
   Hephsibah = King Hezekiah (2 Kings 21:1)
   Meshullemeth = King Manasseh (2 Kings 21:19, 20)
   Jedidah = King Amon (2 Kings 21:24; 22:1)
   Hamutal/Nehushta/Zebudah = King Josiah (2 Kings 23:30;
      2 Chron. 36:1)

What prophets wrote about whirlwinds?
   Isaiah (Isa. 5:28)
   Amos (Amos 1:14)
   Jeremiah (Jer. 4:13)
   Nahum (Nahum 1:3)
   Ezekiel (Ezek. 1:4)
   Habakkuk (Hab. 3:14)
   Daniel (Dan. 11:40)
   Zechariah (Zech. 7:14)
   Hosea (Hosea 8:7)

Who were the prophets during the divided kingdom of Israel and Judah?

Ahijah (1 Kings 11:28–30)

Jehu (1 Kings 16:1–7)

Elijah (1 Kings 17–21)

Elisha (1 Kings 19:19–21)

Amos (Amos 7)

Isaiah (2 Kings 20:1–21)

Hosea (Hosea 1:1)

Micah (Micah 1:1)

What prophets served Judah while Israel was exiled or in captivity?

Nahum

Obadiah

Habakkuk

Haggai

Jeremiah

Zechariah

Daniel

Malachi

Which prophets who authored Bible books claimed that the "Word of the Lord" came to them?

Samuel (1 Sam. 15:10)

Jonah (Jonah 1:1)

Isaiah (Isa. 38:4)

Micah (Micah 1:1)

Jeremiah (Jer. 14:1)

Zephaniah (Zeph. 1:1)

Hosea (Hos. 1:1)

Haggai (Hag. 2:20)

Joel (Joel 1:1)

Zechariah (Zech. 1:1)

What prophets are mentioned in the Bible but did not write a book?
  Gad (2 Sam. 24:11)
  Nathan (1 Chron. 29:29)
  Ahijah (1 Kings 14:18)
  Shemaiah (2 Chron. 12:15)
  Jehu (1 Kings 16:12)
  Hananiah (Jer. 28:12)
  Micaiah (1 Kings 22:13)
  Agabus (Acts 21:10)

The term "And the Lord said unto" is used regarding which prophets?
  Samuel (1 Sam. 8:7)
  Jeremiah (Jer. 1:9)
  Ahijah (1 Kings 14:5)
  Hosea (Hos. 1:2)
  Elijah (1 Kings 19:15)
  Amos (Amos 7:8)
  Jehu (2 Kings 10:30)
  Zechariah (Zech. 11:15)

Who are the Levites that explain the readings from the Book of Law?
Nehemiah 8:7–8

Jeshua	Kelita
Shabbethai	Akkub
Bani	Azariah
Hodijah	Jozabad
Sherebiah	Hanan
Maaseiah	Pelaiah
Jamin	

What men are mentioned as the "Seer?"
  Samuel (1 Sam. 9:9)
  Zadok (2 Sam. 15:27)
  Gad (2 Sam. 24:11)
  Heman (1 Chron. 25:5)
  Iddo (2 Chron. 9:29)
  Hanani (2 Chron. 16:7)
  Asaph (2 Chron. 29:30)
  Jeduthun (2 Chron. 35:15)

Who does the Bible mention as being a high priest?
  Melchizedek (Gen. 14:18)
  Hilkiah (2 Kings 22:8)
  Eliashib (Neh. 3:1)
  Josedech (Hag. 2:2)
  Caiaphas (Matt. 26:3)
  Abiathar (Mark 2:26)
  Annas (Acts 4:6)
  Ananias (Acts 23:2)
  Jesus Christ (Heb. 6:20)

What priests blew a trumpet?
  Phinehas (Num. 31:6)
  Amasai (1 Chron. 15:24)
  Zadok (1 Kings 1:39)
  Zechariah (1 Chron. 15:24)
  Shebaniah (1 Chron. 15:24)
  Benaiah (1 Chron. 15:24)
  Jehoshaphat (1 Chron. 15:24)
  Eliezer (1 Chron. 15:24)
  Nethaneel (1 Chron. 15:24)

Who was a prophetess mentioned in the Bible?
  Miriam (Exod. 15:20)
  Isaiah's wife (Isa. 8:3)
  Deborah (Judges 4:4)
  Four daughters of Philip (Act 21:9)
  Huldah (2 Kings 22:14)
  Anna (Luke 2:36)
  Noadiah (Neh. 6:14)

Who were the Judges of Israel?
  Othniel (Judges 3:7–11)
  Jephthah (Judges 10:6–12)
  Ehud (Judges 3:12–30)
  Ibzan (Judges 12:8–10)
  Gideon (Judges 6:1–8)
  Elon (Judges 12:11, 12)
  Tola (Judges 10:1, 2)
  Abdon (Judges 12:13–15)
  Jair (Judges 10:3–5)
  Samson (Judges 15:20)

What ten judges judged Israel the longest?
  Ehud, eighty years (Judges 3:15, 30)
  Jair, twenty-two years (Judges 10:3)
  Othniel, forty years (Judges 3:9–11)
  Samson, twenty years (Judges 13:24; 16:31)
  Deborah and Barak, forty years (Judges 4:4, 6; 5:31)
  Abdon, eight years (Judges 12:13–15)
  Gideon, forty years (Judges 8:28)
  Ibzan, seven years (Judges 12:8–10)
  Tola, twenty-three years (Judges 10:1–2)
  Jepthah, six years (Judges 11:1, 11; 12:7)

Religious Matters

What are the Ten Commandments of God? Exodus 20:2–18

    Do not worship other gods

    Do not worship idols

    Do not misuse God's name

    Remember the Sabbath day and keep it holy

    Honor you parents

    Do not murder

    Do not commit adultery

    Do not steal

    Do not lie/bear false witness

    Do not covet

The Bible talks about being "Justified by" what?

    Justified by the faith of Jesus Christ (Gal. 2:16)

    Justified by faith without deeds of the law (Rom. 3:28)

    Justified by His grace (Titus 3:7)

    Justified by His blood (Rom. 5:9)

    Justified by works (James 2:25)

What things doth the Lord hate? Proverbs 6:16–19

Proud looks

Lying tongue

Hands that shed innocent blood

Hearts that deviseth wicked imaginations

Being swift in running to mischief

A false witness that speaketh lies

Those soweth discord among brethren

What are the biblical qualifications and responsibilities of a deacon?
1 Timothy 3:8–13 (NKJV)

Must be reverent

Faithful with a pure conscience

Not double-tongued

Husband of one wife

Not given to much wine

Ruling their children and their own houses well

Not greedy for money

The book of Romans lists what items of improper conduct that are deserving of death? Romans 1:29–31

Filled with unrighteousness, wickedness

Backbiters, haters of God, covenant breakers

Fornication

Covetousness, full of envy

Inventors of evil things

Maliciousness

Disobedient to parents

Murder

Without understanding, implacable

Spiteful

Proud, boasters

Without natural affection, unmerciful

What works of the flesh are listed in Galatians 5:19–21?

Adultery/Fornication

Envy

Uncleanness/Lasciviousness

Emulations/Striving

Idolatry

Seditions/Heresies/revellings

Sorcery/witchcraft

Murder

Hatred/wrath

Drunkenness

What are the characteristics of love according to 1 Corinthians 13? (NIV)

Is patient

Is not self-seeking/not easily angered

Is kind

Keeps no record of wrongs

Does not envy/does not boast

Does not delight in evil but rejoices with truth

Does not dishonor others

Always protects/trusts/perseveres/hopes

Is not proud/is not rude

Never fails

What does Psalms say about a man's tongue?

Makes mischief (Ps. 5:9)

Speaks vanity (Ps. 5:9)

Talks of judgment (Ps. 37:30)

Speaks Deceit (Ps. 50:19)

Speaks proud things (Ps. 12:3)

Lies (Ps. 52:3)

Backbites (Ps. 15:3)

Is False (Ps. 120:3)

What are the guidelines for Christian living for slaves? Titus 2:9, 10 (NIV)

> Slave is subject to their masters in everything
> Do not steal from their masters
> Try to please their master
> Show that they can be fully trusted
> Not to talk back to their master
> Will make the teaching about God appealing in every way

What are the guidelines for Christian living for aged men and women?
Titus 2:2, 3 (NIV)

> Be temperate
> Worthy of respect
> Be reverent in the way they live
> Self-controlled
> Not to be slanderers
> Sound in faith, love, and endurance
> Not addicted to much wine
> To teach what is good

What are the guidelines for Christian living for younger men and women?
Titus 2:4–8 (NIV)

> Love their husbands and children
> Be subject to their husbands
> Be self-controlled and pure
> In everything set an example by doing what is good
> Be busy at home
> Show integrity and seriousness
> Be kind
> Use clean language that no one can criticize

What instruction is given concerning the elders in the church? Titus 1:5–9

    Be blameless, just, holy

    Not given to wine

    Husband of one wife

    Not greedy for money

    Having faithful children

    Be hospitable and a lover of good

    A steward of God, not self-willed

    Sober-minded, self-controlled

    Not quick-tempered, not violent

    Holding fast the faithful word

Jesus told his disciples what defiles a man in Matthew 15:18–20?

    Evil thoughts

    Thefts

    Murders

    False witness

    Adulteries

    Blasphemies

    Fornications

Paul advised the Colossians to get rid of what earthly vices? Colossians 3:5, 8

    Fornication

    Anger, wrath

    Uncleanness

    Malice

    Evil desires

    Blasphemy

    Covetousness

    Filthy communication out of your mouth

    Idolatry

    Lies

Paul tells us to think on what things in Philippians 4:8?
  True
  Pure
  Honest
  Lovely
  Just
  Good report

In 1 Corinthians 5:9–11 Paul warms us not to associates with people who are what?
  Fornicators
  Idolators
  Covetous
  Revilers
  Extortioners
  Drunkards

What must you put away without malice according to Paul? Ephesians 4:31
  Bitterness
  Wrath
  Anger
  Clamour
  Evil speaking

Peter enumerates what qualities that we need for living a godly life?
2 Peter 1:5–7

  Giving all diligence
  Self-control
  Perseverance
  Faith and virtue
  Godliness
  Virtue
  Knowledge
  Brotherly kindness
  Love

What are the characteristic of the unrighteous who shall not inherit the kingdom of God? 1 Corinthians 6:9–11

Fornicators

Thieves

Idolaters

Covetous

Adulterers

Drunkards

Effeminate

Revilers

Abusers of themselves

Extortioners

What will be the prominent sins of people in the last days? 2 Timothy 3:2–4

Lovers of themselves

Unforgiving

Slanderers

Lovers of money

Without self-control, brutal

Boasters, proud, blasphemers

Despisers of good

Traitors

Disobedient to parents

Headstrong, haughty

Unthankful

Unholy

Unloving

Lovers of pleasure rather than lovers of God

What are the qualifications of an overseer according to Paul? 1 Timothy 3:1–7

Blameless

Husband of one wife

Not given to wine

Temperate

Gentle

Not violent

Not quarrelsome

Sober-minded

Of good behavior

Not greedy for money, not covetous

Hospitable

One who rules his own house well

Able to teach

Having his children in submission with all reverence

What does Paul say are desirable characteristics for older men?
Titus 2:2 (NKJV)

Sober

Sound in faith

Reverent

Sound in love

Temperate

Sound in patience

What does Paul say are desirable characteristics for older women?
Titus 2:3–5 (NKJV)

Reverent in behavior

To love their children

Not slanderers

To be discreet *(self-controlled)*

Not given to much wine

Chaste *(pure)*

Good *(kind)*

Teachers of good things

Homemakers

Obedient to their own husband

What are the practices of man that are worthy of death according to Romans 1:29–31 (NKJV)?

Sexual immorality

Wickedness

Haters of God

Violent

Covetousness

Maliciousness

Envious

Proud, boasters

Murder

Strife

Inventors of evil things

Disobedient

Deceit

Undiscerning

Untrustworthy

Whisperers, backbiters

Unloving, unforgiving, unmerciful

What should not be done to the widows and fatherless?

Not to be afflicted (Exod. 22:22)

Not to be slayed (Ps. 94:6)

Not to be deprived of raiment (Deut. 24:17)

Not to be made prey of (Isa. 10:2)

Not to be sent away empty (Job 22:9)

Treated not with violence (Jer. 22:3)

Not to take pledges from them (Job 24:3)

Not to be vexed (Ezek. 22:7)

Do not disappoint (Job 31:16)

Do not oppress (Zech. 7:10)

What should be done for the widows and fatherless?

Allowed to share in our blessings (Deut. 24:19–21)

Relieved by their church (1 Tim. 5:16)

Do good to them (Job 24:21)

Visited in time of affliction (James 1:27)

Cause them joy (Job 29:13)

Do not pervert judgments (Deut. 27:19)

Plead for them (Isa. 1:17)

They should be honored (1 Tim. 5:3)

What are the "good" traits of man that the Bible describes?

Good courage (Deut. 31:6)

Good to sing praises (Ps. 147:1)

Good understanding (1 Sam. 25:3)

Good name (Prov. 22:1)

Good words (1 Kings 12:7)

Good cheer (Matt. 9:2)

Good works (Neh. 2:18)

Good manners (1 Cor. 15:33)

Good spirit (Neh. 9:20)

Good conscience (1 Tim. 1:5)

In what ways can young men set an example to believers? 1 Timothy 4:12

In word

In spirit

In conversation/conduct

In faith

In charity

In purity

What does the "Lord God require of thee?"

Fear the Lord they God (Deut. 10:12)

Walk in all His ways (Deut. 10:12)

To love Him (Deut. 10:12)

Serve the Lord God with all thy heart and soul (Deut. 10:12)

Hearken unto my words (Deut. 18:19)

To do justly (Micah 6:8)

To love mercy (Micah 6:8)

To walk humbly with God, Micah 6:8

What are the "Spiritual Gifts" according to Paul in Romans 12:6–8?

Ministry

Mercy

Teaching

Exhortation

Leadership

What "Spiritual Gifts" are found in 1 Corinthians 12:8–11?

Word of wisdom

Prophecy

Word of Knowledge

Discerning spirit

Faith

Different kinds of tongues

Gifts of healing

Interpretation of tongues

The working of miracles

How are human emotions expressed in the Bible with the term "Spirit of ...?"

Spirit of jealousy (Num. 5:14)

Spirit of grace and of supplications (Zech. 12:10)

Spirit of heaviness (Isa. 61:3)

Spirit of fear (2 Tim. 1:7)

What human attributes that are not emotions are expressed by the term "Spirit of ...?"

Spirit of wisdom and understanding (Isa. 11:2)

Spirit of counsel and might (Isa. 11:2)

Spirit of knowledge and of the fear of the Lord (Isa. 11:2)

Spirit of the humble (Isa. 57:15)

Spirit of judgment (Isa. 28:6)

Spirit of infirmity (Luke 13:11)

Spirit of truth (John 14:17)

Spirit of bondage (Rom. 8:15)

Spirit of meekness (1 Cor. 4:21)

Spirit of your mind (Eph. 4:23)

Nature

What did God create on each day?

Day 1: Light and separated it from darkness (Gen. 1:1–5)

Day 2: Sky/firmament (Gen. 1:6–8)

Day 3: Land, seas and plants (Gen. 1:9–13)

Day 4: Sun, moon, and stars (Gen. 1:14–19)

Day 5: Fish and birds (Gen. 1:20–23)

Day 6: Animals and man (Gen. 1:24–31)

Day 7: Day of rest (Gen. 2:1–3)

What non-edible fruit bearing trees are mentioned in the Bible?

Cedar/Aloes (2 Sam. 5:11)

Fir (2 Chron. 2:8)

Mulberry (2 Sam. 5:23)

Willows (Job 40:22)

Almug/Hyssop (1 King 10:11)

Cacia (Isa. 41:19)

Sycamore (1 Kings 10:27)

Pine/Myrtle (Isa. 60:13)

Juniper (1 Kings 19:4)

Oak (Jer. 11:2)

What Heavenly bodies are mentioned in the Bible?
Arcturus (Job 9:9)
Pleiades (Job 9:9)
Orion (Job 9:9)
Earth (Gen. 1:17)
Jupiter (Acts 19:35)
Moon (Gen. 37:9)
Stars (Gen. 37:9)
Sun (Gen. 37:9)

Where did the angel pour the seven bowls for the seven last plagues?
Earth (Rev. 16:2)
Sea (Rev. 16:3)
Rivers and Fountains (Rev. 16:4)
Sun (Rev. 16:8)
Seat of the Beast (Rev. 16:10)
Great River Euphrates (Rev. 16:12)
Air (Rev. 16:17)

David uses similes to compare himself to what?
Poured out like water (Ps. 22:14)
Like an owl of the desert (Ps. 102:6)
Like a broken vessel (Ps. 31:12)
Withered like grass (Ps. 102:11)
Like a green olive tree (Ps. 52:8)
Tossed up and down as locusts (Ps. 109:23)
As a man with no strength (Ps. 88:4)
Gone like the shadow (Ps. 109:23)
Like a pelican of the wilderness (Ps. 102:6)
Becomes like a bottle in the smoke (Ps. 119:83)

Bible Occupations

What agricultural operations are mentioned in the Bible?
Plowing (Isa. 28:24)
Sowing (Gen. 47:23)
Reaping/Harvesting (1 Sam. 6:13)
Threshing (Lev. 26:5)
Winnowing (Isa. 30:24)

What are Biblical business-related occupations? (NKJV)
Messenger (Gen. 32:3)
Trader (Gen.37:28)
Moneychanger (Matt. 21:12)
Treasurer (Ezra 1:8)
Scribe (2 Sam. 8:17)
Weaver (Exod. 35:35)
Tax collector (Matt. 5:46)

What farm and manual labor occupations are mentioned in the Bible?

Herdsmen (Amos 1:1)

Servant (Gen. 9:26)

Hunter (Gen. 10:9)

Labourer (1 Tim. 5:18)

Plower (Ps. 129:3)

Mason (1 Chron. 14:1)

Reaper (Amos 9:13)

Stonesquarer (1 Kings 5:18)

Shepherd (Ps. 23:1)

What are king's court and food service related occupations of the Bible?

Baker (Gen. 40:5)

Butler (Gen. 40:5)

Cupbearer (Neh. 1:11)

Barber (Ezek. 5:1)

Chamberlains (Esther 6:2)

Grinders (Eccles. 12:3)

Cook (1 Sam. 8:13)

What military related occupations are mentioned in the Bible?

Armourbearer (1 Sam. 16:21)

Guard (Gen. 37:36)

Soldier/Warrior (2 Tim. 2:3)

Watcher (Dan. 4:13)

What are professional and medically related occupations talked about in the Bible?

Embalmer (Gen. 50:2)

Instructor (Rom. 2:20)

Midwife (Gen. 35:17)

Lawyers (Luke 11:46)

Nurse (Gen. 35:8)

Pastor (Jer. 17:16)

Physician (Col. 4:14)

Preacher (Eccles. 1:1)

Counselor (1 Chron. 27:33)

Priest (Exod. 29:1)

What trade and arts-based occupations are mentioned in the Bible?

Carpenter (Matt. 13:55)

Potter (Isa. 64:8)

Coppersmith (2 Tim. 4:14)

Sailor (Rev. 18:17)

Embroiderer (Exod. 35:35)

Silversmith (Acts 19:24)

Goldsmith (Isa. 41:7)

Singer (Hab. 3:19)

Musician (Rev. 18:22)

Tentmaker (Acts 18:3)

Biblical Events

According to Ecclesiastes 3, to everything there is a season. Fill in the blank: "a time to…"

… be born, plant

… get, keep

… kill, break down

… rend

… weep, mourn

… keep silence

… cast away stones

… love

… embrace

… war

… die

… refrain from embracing

… pluck up that which is planted

… lose, cast away

… heal, build up

… sow

… laugh, dance

… speak

… gather stones together

… hate, peace

Where in the Bible does the "Primeval Light" make appearances?
(Shekinah Glory)
>Gate of Eden, flaming swords (Gen 3:24)
>Wilderness tabernacle (Exod. 40:34)
>Moses and the burning bush (Exod. 3:2)
>The temple in Jerusalem (2 Chron. 5:14)
>Bank of the Red Sea, between Pharaoh and Israel (Exod. 14:24)
>Bethlehem (Luke 2:9)
>Pillar of fire in the wilderness (Exod. 13:21)
>Mount of Transfiguration (Matt 17:2)
>Sinai (Exod. 19:18; 24:17)
>Paul on the road to Damascus (Acts 9:3)

What were the feasts of Bible times?
>Feast of Unleavened Bread (Passover) (Exod. 12:17)
>Feast of Weeks (Exod. 34:22)
>Feast of Harvest (Exod. 23:16)
>Feast of Ingathering (Exod. 23:16)
> Feast of Tabernacles (Lev. 23:34)
>Feast of Dedication (John 10:22)

During what Biblical events did a cloud or clouds appear?
>Elijah prayed for rain (1 Kings 18:44)
>To lead Israel in the desert (Exod. 13:21)
>Jesus was baptised (Matt. 17:5)
>Moses received the Ten Commandments (Exod. 34:5)
>Jesus taken up to heaven (Acts 1:9)
>Lord called Aaron and Miriam to the tent (Num. 12:5)
>Living righteous ascend to heaven to meet the Lord (1 Thess. 4:17)
>Cloud covered the tabernacle after building (Num. 9:15)

What things happened behind closed doors?

Lot's visitors smote the men with blindness (Gen. 19:10, 11)

Kept Shemiah alive from Sanballat (Neh. 6:10)

Israelites saved from death at Passover (Exod. 12:7)

Prayed (Matt. 6:6)

Ehud killed Eglon, king of Moab (Judges 3:17–23)

Coming of the bridegroom and the 5 wise virgins (Matt. 25:9–11)

Oil filling up the vessels (2 Kings 4:4)

Children sleeping (Luke 11:7)

Elisha raised the dead boy (2 Kings 4:21)

Jesus stood in the midst of the disciples (John 20:19–26)

On what occasion or in what places was there "no water?"

Joseph cast into waterless pit (Gen. 37:24)

The Lord's power to punish Israel with not sending water (Isa. 44:12)

Israelites in the Wilderness of Sin (Exod. 15:22)

Jeremiah cast into a dry dungeon (Jer. 38:6)

Encamped at Rephidim (Num. 33:14)

Jesus given no water to wash His feet (Luke 7:44)

Israelites marched 7 days to Moab (2 Kings 3:9)

When is "stand still" mentioned in the Bible?

Israel by Red Sea (Exod. 14:13)

Jonathan and his armor bearer (1 Sam. 14:9)

Priest carrying the Ark at the Jordan (Joshua 3:8)

Ahimaaz (2 Sam. 18:30)

Sun (Joshua 10:12)

Jehoshaphat's army (2 Chron. 20:17)

Saul (1 Sam. 9:27)

Job (Job 37:14)

What things happened to Paul at night?

Vision at Macedonia (Acts 16:9)

Brethren sent away and escape to Berea (Acts 17:10)

Singing and praising God (Acts 16:26)

Soldiers brought Paul by night to Antipatris (Acts 23:31)

Baptized the prison guard and family (Acts 16:33)

Angel spoke to Paul, who had a shipwreck (Acts 27:23)

Vision in Corinth (Acts 18:9)

Paul prayed (2 Tim. 1:3)

What things did the disciples do at night?

Sailing and saw Jesus walking on the sea (Matt. 14:25)

Fishing (Luke 5:5)

Partaking of the Last Supper (Matt. 26:20)

Sleeping while Jesus prayed (Matt. 26:40)

Followed and watched Jesus (Matt. 26:34)

Peter and other apostles released from prison by an angel (Acts 5:19)

Paul escaped by wall in a basket (Acts 9:25)

What notable ten-day events are recorded in the Bible?

"Let Rebekah stay with us for ten days, then she can go" (Gen. 24:55)

Lord smote Nabal after ten days (1 Sam. 25:38)

Lord came to Jeremiah in a vision after ten days (Jer. 42:7)

Daniel's request for ten days test of their diet (Dan. 1:12)

Daniel and friends were smarter and stronger after ten days of test (Dan. 1:14)

What notable twelve-day or twelve-month events are recorded in the Bible?

Ahira's, prince of tribe of Naphtali's, turn to offer sacrifice
(Num. 7:78)

Priest and Levites departed Ahava River to Jerusalem
(Ezra 8:30, 31)

The word of the Lord came to Ezekiel (Ezek. 29:1)

Heldai of Othniel served as captain to King David (1 Chron. 27:15)

King's command to kill all the Jews (Esther 9:1)

King Jehoiachin of Judah brought out of Babylon prison (Jer. 52:31)

What are notable life events of people when they were thirty years old?

Shelah's son Eber was born (Gen. 11:14)

Saul became King (1 Sam. 13:1, NIV)

Peleg, son Reu, was born (Gen. 11:18)

David became King (2 Sam. 5:4)

Serug's son, Nahor, was born (Gen. 11:22)

Levites start serving the temple (1 Chron. 23:3)

Joseph began serving the king of Egypt (Gen. 41:46)

Jesus began teaching (Luke 3:23)

What are the 40 days and 40 nights events of the Bible?

God flooded the earth (Gen. 7:4)

Goliath insulted Israel's army (1 Sam. 17:16)

Noah was in the ark (Gen. 8:6)

Elijah hiding at Mt. Horeb (1 Kings 19:8)

Joseph embalmed his father (Gen. 50:3)

Ezekiel bore the iniquity of Judah (Ezek. 4:6)

Moses at Mt. Sinai with God (Exod. 24:18)

Jonah preached at Nineveh (Jonah 3:4)

Joshua and Caleb spying the land (Num. 13:25)

Jesus fasting in the wilderness (Matt. 4:2)

Days before David arrived to his brothers (1 Sam. 17:16)

Days the disciples were with Jesus after resurrection (Acts 1:3)

Moses fell begs the Lord not to destroy Israel (Deut. 9:25)

What men were forty years old when they did special things and what did they do?

Isaac was 40 when he took Rebekah to wife (Gen. 25:20)

Esau was 40 when he took Judith to wife (Gen. 26:34)

Joshua was 40 when he spied out the land (Joshua 14:7)

Ishbosheth was 40 when he began to reign over Israel (2 Sam. 2:10)

Moses was 40 when he visited his brethren, the children of Israel (Acts 7:23)

During the lives of which Bible people was there famine?

Abraham and Isaac (Gen. 12:10)

Elisha (2 Kings 4:38)

Jacob and Joseph (Gen. 41:50–56)

Nebuchadnezzar (Jer. 52:1–6)

Naomi's family (Ruth 1:1)

David (2 Sam. 21:1)

King Ahab (Elijah) (1 Kings 17:1)

Claudius Caesar (Acts 11:28)

Joseph (Acts 7:11)

What earthquakes are recorded in the Bible?

God at Mt. Sinai with Moses (Exod. 19:18)

God at the Mount with Elijah (1 Kings 19:11)

During King Uzziah's reign of Judah (Zech. 14:5)

Jesus at the cross (Matt. 27:54)

Angel rolled out the stone at Jesus' tomb (Matt. 28:2–4)

Peter in the prison cell (Acts 16:26)

Angel opened the sixth seal (Rev. 6:12)

What leaves of a tree are mentioned in the Bible?

Fig leaves (Gen. 3:7)

Olive leaf (Gen. 8:11)

Oak leaf (Isa. 1:30)

Tree of Life leaves (Rev. 22:2)

God planted what trees in the wilderness? Isaiah 41:19

Cedar

Fir

Shittah/Acacia

Pine

Myrtle

Box/cypress tree

Oil/Olive tree

What providence did God have for Israel in the Wilderness?

Salvation—crossing the Red Sea (Exod. 14:27–30)

Clouds as shade by day (Exod. 13:21)

Fire as light by night (Exod. 13:21)

Water from Marah (Exod. 15:23)

Health to those who obey (Exod. 15:26)

Quails for meat (Exod. 16:13)

Manna for food (Exod. 16:35–36)

What are are the names of Jewish months in the Bible?

Nisan (1) (Esther 3:7)

Zif (2) (1 Kings 6:1)

Sivan (3) (Esther 8:9)

Elul (6) (Neh. 6:15)

Ethanim (7) (1 Kings 8:2)

Bul (8) (1 Kings 6:38)

Chisleu (9) (Zech. 7:1)

Tebeth (10) (Esther 2:16)

Sebat (11) (Zech. 1:7)

Adar (12) (Esther 3:7)

Abib (Exod. 23:15)

Food

What seasonings, spices, and herbs are mentioned in the Bible?

Salt (Lev. 2:13)   Saffron (Song of Sol. 4:14)

Anise (Matt. 23:23)   Coriander (Exod. 16:31)

Mustard (Matt. 13:31)   Calamus (Song of Sol. 4:14)

Garlic (Num. 11:5)   Mint (Matt. 23:23)

Cinnamon (Exod. 30:23)   Onion (Num. 11:5)

What vegetables and legumes are listed in the Bible?

Beans (Ezek. 4:9)

Leeks (Num. 11:5)

Lentils (Ezek. 4:9)

Cucumbers (Num. 11:5)

Fitches (peas) (Ezek. 4:9)

Onion (Num. 11:5)

Gourd (Num. 11:5)

What grains are mentioned in the Bible?
Barley (Ezek. 4:9)
Spelt (Ezek. 4:9, NKJV)
Wheat (Ezek. 4:9)
Corn (Gen. 42:3)
Millet (Ezek. 4:9)
Flax (Exod. 9:31, NKJV)

What non-vegetable, fruit, grain, or legume foods and drinks are mentioned in the Bible?
Eggs (Job 6:6)
Olive oil (Ezek.45:14)
Grape juice (Num. 6:3 NKJV)
Vinegar (Ruth 2:14)
Honey (Jer. 41:8)
Wine (Num. 6:3)
Locust (Lev. 11:22)

What fruits and nuts are mentioned in the Bible?
Fig (Prov. 27:18)
Almond (Gen. 43:11)
Olive (Neh. 9:25)
Raisin (1 Sam. 30:12)
Grape (Deut. 23:24)
Pomegranates (Deut. 8:8)
Melon (Num. 11:5)
Apple (Joel 1:12)
Sycamore (Amos 7:14)

What edible things were sold or bought during Bible times?

Ass's head (2 Kings 6:25)

Sweet cane (Isa. 43:24)

Dove's dung (2 Kings 6:25)

Sparrows (Matt. 10:29)

Fine flour and barley (2 Kings 7:1, 16)

Doves (Matt. 21:12)

Lamb (2 Sam. 12:3)

Sweet spices (Mark 16:1)

Oxen (2 Sam. 24:24)

What edible fruit bearing trees are mentioned in the Bible?

Hazel (Gen. 30:37)

Chesnut (Gen. 30:37)

Pomegranate (1 Sam. 14:2)

Apple (Song of Sol. 2:3)

Olive (Deut. 24:20)

Almond (Eccles. 12:5)

Palm (Judges 4:5)

Fig (Judges 9:10)

Pine (Isa. 60:13)

What animal meats are clean and can be eaten according to the Bible?

Oxen (Deut. 14:4)

Goat (Deut. 14:4)

Lamb (Amos 6:4)

Calf (Gen. 18:8)

Venison (Gen. 25:28)

What dairy products are mentioned in the Bible?

Butter (Isa. 7:15)

Cheese (1 Sam. 17:18)

Curds (Job 10:10)

Milk (Isa. 7:22)

What foods did the Israelites remember eating in Egypt? Numbers 11:5

    Fish

    Leeks

    Cucumbers

    Onions

    Melons

    Garlic

Bible Personalities

Who were the first ten men to live on Earth?

Adam (Gen. 5:3–5)

Cain (Gen. 4:1)

Abel (Gen. 4:2)

Seth (Gen. 5:6–7)

Enos (Gen. 5:9–11)

Cainan (Gen. 5:12–14)

Mahalaleel (Gen. 5:15–17)

Jared (Gen. 5:18–20)

Enoch (Gen. 5:21–24)

Methuselah (Gen. 5:25–29)

Who had both their birth and death recorded in the Bible?

Abel (Gen. 4:2 and Gen. 4:8)

Jacob (Gen. 25:21–26 and Gen. 49:33)

Seth (Gen. 4:25 and Gen. 5:8)

Er (Gen. 38:3 and Gen. 46:12)

Terah (Gen. 11:24 and Gen. 11:32)

Moses (Exod. 2:2 and Deut. 34:5)

Ishmael (Gen. 16:4– 15 and Gen. 25:17)

Samuel (1 Sam. 1:20 and 1 Sam. 25:1)

Isaac (Gen. 21:2 and Gen. 35:29)

Solomon (2 Sam. 12:24 and 1 Kings 11:40)

What liars are found in the Bible?

Serpent/Satan (Gen. 3:4, 5)
Rahab (Joshua 2:5)
Cain (Gen. 4:9)
Samson (Judges 16:11)
Abraham (Gen. 12:19)
Michal (1 Sam. 19:17)
Sarah (Gen. 18:15)
Gehazi (2 Kings 5:21)
Isaac (Gen. 26:6–8)
Hazael (2 Kings 8:14–15)
Rachel (Gen. 31:35)
Micaiah (2 Chron. 18:14–22)
Joseph's brethren
  (Gen. 37:32)
Peter (Luke 22:54–57)
Potiphar's wife (Gen. 39:17)
Ananias and Sapphira
  (Acts 5:1–9)

Who were un-named people found at a well?

Abraham's servant (Gen. 24:12, 13)
Woman in Bahurim (2 Sam. 17:17–19)
Daughters of the Priest of Midian (Exod. 2:15–21)
Three mighty men of David (2 Sam. 23:15–16)
Shepherds (Exod. 2:15–21)
Woman of Samaria (John 4:6–10)

What named people were found at a well?

Hagar (Gen. 21:17–19)
Jonathan (2 Sam. 17:17–19)
Ahimaaz (2 Sam. 17:17–19)
Rebekah (Gen. 24:15)
Rachel (Gen. 29:2–11)
Jacob (Gen. 29:2–11)
Uzziah (2 Chron. 26:9–10)
Jeremiah (Jer. 38:6)
Moses (Exod. 2:15–21)
Jesus (John 4:6)

Who were the sons of Abraham with Sarah, Hagar, and Keturah?
1 Chronicles 1:28, 32

Ishmael	Zimran
Medan	Ishbak
Isaac	Jokshan
Midian	Shuah

Who are the sons of Nahor and Milcah? Genesis 22:22–24

Huz	Chesed
Pildash	Tebah
Buz	Hazo
Jidlaph	Gaham
Kemuel	Thahash
Bethuel	Maachah

Who talked to Job during his affliction?

Job's wife (Job 2:9)
Eliphaz the Temanite (Job 15:2)
Bildad the Shuhite (Job 8:3)
Zophar the Naamathite (Job 11:3)
Elihu the Buzite (Job 36:3)
God (Job 42:7)

What people were responsible for the construction or re-construction of the Jerusalem Temple?

King David (2 Sam. 7:1–3)
Darius the Great (Ezra 6)
King Solomon (1 Kings 6)
Zerubbabel (Haggai 1:1–15)
King Jehoash of Judah (2 Kings 12:4, 5)
Artaxerxes I of Persia (Ezra 7:1)
Cyrus the Great (Ezra 5:13)

Who refused to eat or who did not eat bread?

 Egyptians (Gen. 43:32)

 Man of God (1 Kings 13:8)

 Moses (Exod. 34:28)

 Ahab (1 Kings 21:4)

 Angel visiting Manoah (Judges 13:16)

 Ezra (Ezra 10:6)

 Saul (1 Sam. 28:20)

 Ezekiel (Ezek. 24:17–19)

 David (2 Sam. 12:17)

Who baked or kneaded bread in the Bible?

 Abraham/Sarah (Gen. 18:4–6)

 Woman of Endor (1 Sam. 28:24)

 Lot (Gen. 19:3)

 Tamar (2 Sam. 13:8)

 Rebekah (Gen. 27:17)

 Zarephath woman (1 Kings 17:13)

 Israelites before leaving Egypt (Exod. 12:39)

Who had a body part other than a head cut off?

 Adoni-Bezek = thumbs and big toes (Judges 1:6)

 David's spy = half of beard (2 Sam. 10:4)

 Samson = eyes and hair (Judges 16:21)

 Malcus = ear (Matt. 26:51)

 Baanah = hands and feet (2 Sam. 4:8–12)

 Paul = hair (Acts 18:18)

 Rechab = hands and feet (2 Sam. 4:8–12)

What men had their heads cut off?

Oreb (Judges 7:24–25)

Zeeb (Judges 7:24–25)

Ishbosheth (2 Sam. 4:8)

Sheba (2 Sam. 20:22)

Goliath (1 Sam. 15:51)

John the Baptist (Matt. 14:10)

King Saul and sons (1 Sam. 31:8–10; 1 Chron. 10:8–10)

Men that joined unto Baal-peor (Num. 25:4–5)

Sisera (Judges 5:26)

Ahab's 70 sons (2 Kings 10:1, 7)

What men had children with a female slave?

Nahor = Reumah (Gen. 22:23–24)

Abraham = Hagar and Keturah (Gen. 25:12; 1 Chron. 1:32)

Eliphaz = Timna (Gen. 36:12)

Jacob = Bilhah and Zilpah (Gen. 37:2)

Saul = Rizpah (2 Sam. 3:7)

Caleb = Ephah and Maachah (1 Chron. 2:46, 48)

What men had unidentified concubine(s)?

Gideon (Judges 8:31)

Manasseh (1 Chron. 7:14)

David (2 Sam. 5:13)

Rehoboam (2 Chron. 11:18–23)

Solomon (1 Kings 11:3)

King Xerxes (Esther 2:14)

Belshazzar (Dan. 5:2)

Who had significant events last for ten years of their life?

Hagar lived with Abram and become 2nd wife (Gen. 16:3)

Elon judged Israel for 10 years (Judges 12:11)

Naomi lived in Moab before going back to Judah (Ruth 1:4)

Manahem reigned over Israel (2 Kings 15:17)

Asa's 10 years of peace in Judah during his reign (2 Chron. 14:1)

What Bible characters "hate" or were "hated?"

Esau hated Jacob (Gen. 27:41)

Rachel hated Leah (Gen. 29:31)

Brothers hated Joseph (Gen. 37:5)

Amnon hated Tamar (2 Sam. 13:15)

Absalom hated Amnon (2 Sam. 13:22)

The King of Israel hated Micaiah, son of Imlah (1 Kings 22:8)

Who was angry or had "kindled anger" against someone?

Esau to Jacob (Gen. 27:45)

Jacob to Rachel (Gen. 30:2)

Moses to Pharaoh (Exod. 11:8)

Eliab to David (1 Sam. 17:28)

Saul to Jonathan (1 Sam. 20:30)

Jonathan to Saul (1 Sam. 20:34)

Balak to Balaam (Num. 24:10)

King Ahasuerus to Vashti (Esther 1:11–12)

Zebul to Abimelech (Judges 9:30)

Rezin to son of Remaliah (Isa. 7:4)

With whom was the Lord angry?
  Moses (Exod. 4:14)
  Gideon (Judges 6:39)
  Aaron (Deut. 9:20)
  Uzzah (2 Sam. 6:7)
  Miriam (Num. 12:9)
  Solomon (1 Kings 11:9)
  Balaam (Num. 22:20–23)
  Amaziah (2 Chron. 25:15)
  Israel (Num. 25:3)

Who were the ten oldest patriarchs?
  Methuselah = 969 (Gen. 5:27)
  Jared = 962 (Gen. 5:20)
  Noah = 950 (Gen. 9:29)
  Adam = 930 (Gen. 5:5)
  Seth = 912 (Gen. 5:8)
  Cainan = 910 (Gen. 5:14)
  Enosh = 905 (Gen. 5:11)
  Mahalalel = 895 (Gen. 5:17)
  Lamech = 777 (Gen. 5:31)
  Enoch = 365 (Gen. 5:23)

Who was buried at the cave of Machpelah?
  Sarah (Gen. 23:19)
  Rebecca (Gen. 49:31)
  Abraham (Gen. 25:9)
  Leah (Gen. 49:31)
  Isaac (Gen. 35:29)
  Jacob (Acts 7:15–16)

Who were the first five disciples that Jesus called? Matthew 4:18–22

Simon Peter

Andrew

James

John

Philip

What people in the Bible are associated with the number 100?

Shem begat a son at 100 years old (Gen. 11:10)

Obadiah hid 100 prophets in two caves (1 Kings 18:4)

Arphaxad was born of Shem at 100 years old (Gen. 11:10)

Elisha's servant feed 100 men (2 Kings 4:43)

Abraham begat a son at 100 years old (Gen. 17:17)

Jesus feeds 5,000 in groups of 100 (Mark 6:40)

Who asked Jesus by faith to heal someone?

Nobleman for his son at Cana of Galilee (Matt. 4:46–54)

Roman centurion for servant who was paralyzed (Matt. 8:5–13)

Jairus for daughter near death and who actually died
(Matt. 9:23–26)

Gentile woman for her demoniac daughter in the region of Tyre and
Sidon (Matt. 15:21–28)

Friends of the paralytic at Capernaum put down through a roof
(Mark 2:2–5)

Father for epileptic son (Mark 9:17–29)

Martha for brother Lazarus (John 11:19–28)

Mary for brother Lazarus (John 11:28–33)

Who in the Old Testament dug wells that were named after them?

Beerlahairoi (Gen. 16:14)   Harod (Judges 7:1)

Abraham (Gen. 21:30)   Sitnah (Gen. 26:21)

Isaac (Gen. 26:18)   Sirah (2 Sam. 3:26)

Nephtoah (Joshua 18:15)   Rehoboth (Gen. 26:22)

Esek (Gen. 26:20)   Uzziah (2 Chron. 26:10)

What men in the Bible had multiple wives?

Solomon: 700 wives, 300 concubines (1 Kings 11:1–7)

Rehoboam: 18 wives, 60 concubines (2 Chron. 11:21)

Abijah: 14 wives (2 Chron. 13:21)

David: 9 wives and more concubines (2 Sam. 5:13)

Caleb: 3 wives, 2 concubines (1 Chron. 2:18–19)

Abraham: 3 wives (Gen. 25:1)

Jacob: 2 wives, 2 handmaids (Gen. 32:22)

King Ahasuerus: 2 wives (Esther)

Esau: 2 wives (Gen. 26:34)

Elkanah: 2 wives (1 Sam. 1:1–2)

Ezra: 2 wives (1 Chron. 4:17–18)

Ashur: 2 wives (1 Chron. 4:5)

Gideon: many wives (Judges 8:30)

What people sat by a gate?

Lot (Gen. 19:1)

David (2 Sam. 18:24; 19:8)

Boaz (Ruth 4:1)

Mordecai (Esther 2:19, 6:10)

Four leprous men (2 Kings 7:3)

King Zedekiah (Jer. 38:7)

Eli (1 Sam. 4:18)

Lazarus (beggar) (Luke 16:20)

Who was at the right side of the pulpit when Ezra read the Law of God?
Nehemiah 8:4

Mattithiah
Urijah
Shema
Hilkiah
Anaiah
Maaseiah

Who was at the left side of the pulpit when Ezra read the Law of God?
Nehemiah 8:4

Pedaiah
Hashbadana
Mishael
Zechariah
Malchiah
Meshullam
Hashum

What Levites explained the law of God read by Ezra? Nehemiah 8:7

Jeshua
Maaseiah
Bani
Kelita
Sherebiah
Azariah
Jamin
Jozabad
Akkub
Hanan
Shabbethai
Pelaiah
Hodiah

Who had dreams in the Bible?

Jacob (Gen. 31:11)

Laban the Syrian (Gen. 31:24)

Joseph (Gen. 37:5)

Pharaoh's butler (Gen. 40:9)

Pharaoh's baker (Gen. 40:16)

Pharaoh (Gen. 41:15)

One of Gideon's soldiers (Judges 7:13)

Solomon (1 Kings 3:5)

Nebuchadnezzar (Dan. 2:1)

Daniel (Dan. 7:1)

Joseph, father of Jesus (Matt. 1:20)

What men's names were changed in the Bible?

Abram = Abraham (Gen. 17:5, 15)

Mattaniah = Zedekiah (2 Kings 24:17)

Jacob = Israel (Gen. 32:28)

Daniel = Belteshazzar (Dan. 1:6–7)

Azariah = Abednego (Dan. 1:7)

Hananiah = Shadrach (Dan. 1:7)

Mishael = Meshach (Dan. 1:7)

Joseph = Zaphnath-paaneah (Gen. 41:45)

Oshea = Joshua (Num. 13:16)

Jedidiah = Solomon (2 Sam. 12:24–25)

Eliakim = Jehoiakim (2 Kings 23:34)

Simon = Peter (John 1:42)

Saul = Paul (Acts 13:9)

Who in the Bible changed someone's name?

God—Abram, Sarai (Gen. 17:2–5, 15)

Jacob—Benoni (Gen. 35:18)

Man (God)—Jacob (Gen. 32:24–28)

Pharaoh—Joseph's (Gen. 41:45)

Men of Ophrah—Gideon (Judges 6:32)

Nathan—Solomon (2 Sam. 12:24–25)

Pharaoh Neco—Eliakim (2 Kings 23:34)

Nebuchadnezzar—Mattaniah (2 Kings 24:17)

Ashpenaz—Daniel (Dan. 1:6–7)

Jesus—Simon (John 1:42)

What men or women were also called by a 2nd name in the Bible?

Esau/Edom (Gen. 25:30)

Hadassah/Esther (Esther 2:7)

Solomon/Jedidiah (2 Samuel 12:24–25)

Levi/Matthew (Matt. 9:9)

Thomas/Didymus (John 11:16)

Joses/Barnabas (Acts 4:35–37)

Saul/Paul (Acts 13:9)

John/Mark (Acts 15:37)

What Bible characters who were not kings worked in a non-Israelite government?

Joseph

Meshach/Mishael

Daniel

Abednego/Azariah

Mordecai

Moses

Cornelius

Esther

Shadrach/Hananiah

What Bible characters stole something?

Jacob (Gen. 31:20)

Micah (Judges 17:2–7)

Rachel (Gen. 31:19)

Achan (Joshua 7:10–26)

Zacchaeus (Luke 19:8)

Judas Iscariot (John 12:4–6)

Barabbas (John 18:40)

What Old Testament Bible characters were prisoners?

Joseph (Gen. 39:20)

Jehoiachin (2 Kings 25:27)

Joseph's brothers
(Gen. 42:19)

Hanani (2 Chron. 16:10)

Samson (Judges 16:21)

Jeremiah (Jer. 38:6–28)

Micaiah (1 Kings 22:27)

Zedekiah (Jer. 52:11)

Hoshea (2 Kings 17:4)

What New Testament Bible characters were prisoners?

John the Baptist (Matt. 11:2)

Barabbas (Matt. 27:16)

Peter (Acts 12:3–19)

Silas (Acts 16:19–40)

Paul (Acts 21:27–40)

What Bible characters impersonated someone or disguised themselves?

Satan (2 Cor. 11:14)

Saul (1 Sam. 28:8)

Sarai (Gen. 12:11–13)

Rebekah (Gen. 26:6–9)

Jacob (Gen. 27:11–13)

David (1 Sam. 22:12–15)

Ahab (1 Kings 22:29–31)

King Josiah (2 Chron. 35:22)

Tamar (Gen. 38:13–19)

Joseph (Gen. 42:7)

Wife of Jeroboam
(1 Kings 14:2)

Un-named prophet
(1 Kings 20:37–39)

What Bible characters were found naked?

Adam and Eve (Gen. 3)

Captives/Prisoners (2 Chron. 28:15)

Noah (Gen. 9:21–23)

Isaiah (Isa. 20:3)

Saul (1 Sam. 19:24)

Micah (Micah 1:8)

Samuel/Prophets (1 Sam. 19:24)

Follower of Jesus (Mark 14:51, 52)

King David (2 Sam. 6:20)

Simon Peter (John 21:7)

What Bible characters were recorded as dancing?

Miriam and virgin Israelite women (Exod. 15:20)

David and Israelite women (1 Sam. 30:16–18)

Israelites—during calf worship (Exod. 32:19)

Prophets/Priest of Baal (1 Kings 18:26)

Jepththah's daughter (Judges 11:34)

Daughters of Shiloh (Judges 21:21)

Daughter of Herodias (Matt. 14:6)

Amalekites (1 Sam. 30:16–18)

House of the prodigal son (Luke 15:25)

Who were fathers of people named Ishmael?

Abraham (Gen. 25:12)

Nethaniah (2 Kings 25:25)

Azel (1 Chron. 8:38)

Jehohanan (2 Chron. 23:1)

Pashur (Ezra 10:22)

What people were recorded eating honey in the Bible?

Samson (2 Sam. 17:29)

Solomon (Song of Sol. 5:1)

Jonathan (1 Sam. 14:27)

John the Baptist (Matt. 3:4)

David (2 Sam. 17:29)

Jesus (Luke 24:42)

What people in the Bible had two daughters?

Lot (Gen. 19:8)

Ahinoam/Saul = Merab and Michal (1 Sam. 14:49)

Laban = Leah and Rachel (Gen. 29:16)

Jesse = Zeruiah and Abigail (1 Chron. 2:16)

Elkanah/Hannah (1 Sam. 2:21)

What men had two wives?

Lamech = Adah and Zillah (Gen. 4:19)

Jehoiada = Jehoshabeath and unnamed wife (2 Chron. 24:3;
2 Chron. 22:11)

Jacob = Leah and Rachel (Gen. 32:22)

King Ahasuerus = Vasti and Ester (Esther 2:17)

Elkanah = Hannah and Peninnah (1 Sam. 1:2)

Esau = Judith and Basemath (Gen. 26:34)

Ashur = Helah and Naarah (1 Chron. 4:5)

Who offered two oxen, five rams, five goats, and five lambs as a sacrifice of offering?

Nahshon the son of Amminadab (Num. 7:17)

Eliasaph the son of Deuel (Num. 7:47)

Nethaneel the son of Zuar (Num. 7:23)

Elishama the son of Ammihud (Num. 7:53)

Eliab the son of Helon (Num. 7:29)

Gamaliel the son of Pedahzur (Num. 7:59)

Elizur the son of Shedeur (Num. 7:35)

Abidan the son of Gideoni (Num. 7:65)

Shelumiel the son of Zurishaddai (Num. 7:41)

Ahiezer the son of Ammishaddai (Num. 7:71)

Pagiel the son of Ocran (Num. 7:77)

Ahira the son of Enan (Num. 7:83)

Who was killed by stoning?

The son of Shelomith (Lev. 24:11–16)

Naboth (1 Kings 21:13–15)

A man picking up woods on the Sabbath day (Num. 15:32–36)

Zechariah the son of Jehoiada (2 Chron. 24:20–22)

Achan and his family (Joshua 7:24–25)

Parable of servant to receive the fruits (Matt. 21:35)

Stephen (Acts 7:58–59)

Adoram (Hadoram) (1 Kings 12:18)

What Bible characters were about to be stoned but were not?

Moses (Exod. 17:4)

Woman accused of adultery (John 8:7)

Jesus (John 10:33)

To whom did the Lord say, "be not afraid?"

Joshua (Joshua 11:6)

Johanan and Jezaniah (Jer. 42:1–11)

Elijah (2 Kings 1:15)

Disciples at sea (Matt. 14:27)

Jehoshaphat (2 Chron. 20:15)

Ruler of the synagogue (Mark 5:36)

People of Zion afraid of the Assyrians (Isa. 10:24)

Paul in his vision (Acts 18:9)

Who was afraid of another person(s)?

King of Moab afraid of Israelites (Num. 22:3)

Hezekiah's officers afraid of the King of the Assyrians (2 Chron. 32:7)

Joshua afraid of King Hazor (Joshua 11:6)

Haman afraid of Esther and the king (Esther 7:6)

King Saul afraid of David (1 Sam. 18:22)

Jeremiah afraid of the Babylonian king (Jer. 42:11)

Elijah afraid of King Ahaziah (2 Kings 1:15)

Disciples afraid of Saul/Paul (Acts 9:26)

What people lived in the land flowing with milk and honey promised to the Israelites? Exodus 3:8, 17

Canaanites

Perizzites

Hittites

Hivites

Amorites

Jebusites

What Bible characters laughed at or mocked someone?

Abraham (Gen. 17:17)

Sanballat the Horonite (Neh. 2:19)

Sarah (Gen. 18:13)

Tobiah the Ammonite official (Neh. 2:19)

Daughters of Zion (2 Kings 19:21)

Geshem the Arabian (Neh. 2:19)

Israelites (2 Chron. 30:10)

People at Jairus' house (Luke 8:53)

Who were King Saul's sons and daughters?

Jonathan (1 Sam. 31:2)

Abinadab (1 Sam. 31:2)

Melchishua (1 Sam. 31:2)

Mephibosheth (2 Sam. 21:8)

Eshbaal (1 Chron. 8:33)

Ishui (1 Sam. 14:49)

Ishbosheth (2 Sam. 2:10)

Armoni (2 Sam. 21:8)

Who were the seven sons of Jesse? 1 Chronicles 2:13–15

Eliab

Raddai

Abinadab

Ozem

Shimea

David

Nethanel

Who are the sons of King David by his named wives? 1 Chronicles 3:1–5

Amnon
Ithream
Daniel or Chileab
Shimea
Absalom
Shobab
Adonijah
Nathan
Shephatiah
Solomon

What sons of King David were born in Hebron? 2 Samuel 3:2–5

Amnon of Ahinoam
Daniel or Chileab of Abigail
Absalom of Maachah
Adonijah of Haggith
Shephatiah of Abital
Ithream of Eglah

What sons of King David were born in Jerusalem? 2 Samuel 5:14–16

Shammuah
Nepheg
Shobab
Japhia
Ibhar
Elishama
Elishua
Eliada
Nathan
Eliphalet
Solomon

What sons of Ishmael were the twelve princes of their nations?
Genesis 25:13–16

Nebajoth
Dumah
Kedar
Massa
Adbeel
Hadar
Mibsam
Tema
Mishma
Jetur

What were the names of the sons to Jacob of Rachel and two hand-maidens? Genesis 35:24–26

Dan
Joseph
Naphtali
Benjamin
Gad
Asher

What were the names of the sons of Jacob and Leah? Genesis 35:23

Reuben
Simeon
Levi
Judah
Issachar
Zebulun

What man said to others, "Fear not?"
Joseph to his brothers (Gen. 43:23)
Absalom to his servant (2 Sam. 13:28)
Moses to the Israelites (Exod. 20:20)
Elijah to widow (1 Kings 17:13)
Joshua to the Israelites (Joshua 10:25)
Elisha to servant (2 Kings 6:16)
Samuel to the Israelites (1 Sam. 12:20)
David to Solomon (1 Chron. 28:20)
Jonathan to David (1 Sam. 23:17)
David to Jonathan (2 Sam. 9:7)

Who said, "Be strong and of good courage?"
Moses (Deut. 31:6)
Hezekiah (2 Chron. 32:7)
God (Joshua 1:6)
Joab (2 Sam. 10:12)
Joshua (Joshua 10:25)
Ezra (Ezra 10:4)
David (1 Chron. 28:20)
Lord (Isa. 41:6)

To whom was "Be strong and of good courage" said?
Twelve spies (Num. 13:20)
Abishai (2 Sam. 10:12)
Joshua (Deut. 31:7)
Solomon (1 Chron. 28:20)
Israelites (Joshua 10:25)
Captains of the Israelites (2 Chron. 32:7)

Give the name of the firstborn child to well-known Bible characters.

Adam/Cain (Gen. 4:1)

Esau/Eliphaz (Gen. 36:15)

Ishmael/Nebajoth (Gen. 25:13)

Joseph/Manasseh (Gen. 41:51)

Isaac/Esau (Gen. 27:32)

Aaron/Nadab (Num. 3:2)

Laban/Leah (Gen. 29:26)

Jesse/Eliab (1 Sam. 17:13)

Jacob/Reuben (Gen. 35:23)

David/Amnon (2 Sam. 3:2)

Who was caught or seen inside a basket?

Moses (Exod. 2:3)

Saul (Acts 9:25)

Paul (2 Cor. 11:33)

A woman (Zech. 5:7)

What people were found under an oak or another tree?

Abraham (Gen. 18:4)

Absalom (2 Sam. 18:9, 10)

Jacob (Gen. 35:4)

Jonathan (1 Chron. 10:12)

Deborah, Rebekah's nurse (Gen. 35:8)

Saul (1 Sam. 14:2)

Joshua (Joshua 24:26)

Elijah (1 Kings 19:5)

Gideon (Judges 6:19)

Job (Job 40:21)

Who were people that were kissed in the Old Testament?

Isaac (Gen. 27:27)

Moses (Exod. 4:27)

Rachel (Gen. 29:11)

Jethro (Exod. 18:7)

Jacob (Gen. 29:13)

Orpah (Ruth 1:9)

Ruth (Ruth 1:9)

Rachel (Gen. 31:55)

Leah (Gen. 31:55)

Naomi (Ruth 1:14)

Ephraim (Gen. 48:10)

Absalom (2 Sam. 14:33)

Manasseh (Gen. 48:10)

David (1 Sam. 10:1)

Jonathan (1 Sam. 20:41)

Amasa (2 Sam. 20:9)

What Bible characters kissed someone?

Jacob kissed Isaac (Gen. 27:26)

Samuel kissed David (1 Sam. 10:1)

Jacob kissed Rachel (Gen. 29:11)

David kissed Jonathan (1 Sam. 20:41)

Laban kissed Jacob (Gen. 29:13)

David kissed Absalom (2 Sam. 14:33)

Laban kissed his daughters and sons (Gen. 31:55)

Absalom kissed his visitors (2 Sam. 15:5)

Esau kissed Jacob (Gen. 33:4)

Joab kissed Amasa (2 Sam. 20:9)

Joseph kissed his brethren (Gen. 45:15)

Naomi kissed daughter-in-law (Ruth 1:9)

Jacob kissed Joseph's sons (Gen. 48:10)

Orpha kissed Naomi (Ruth 1:14)

Joseph kissed his father (Gen. 50:1)

Judas kissed Jesus (Matt. 26:49)

Aaron kissed Moses (Exod. 4:27)

Mary Magdalene kissed Jesus (Luke 7:38)

Moses kissed his father-in-law (Exod. 18:7)

Name famous husband and wife pairs in the Bible.

Adam and Eve (Gen. 3:20)

Moses and Zepporah
(Exod. 18:2)

Isaac and Rebekah
(Gen. 25:20)

Othniel and Achsah
(Joshua 15:16)

Esau and Judith (Gen. 26:34)

Boaz and Ruth (Ruth 4:13)

Jacob and Leah (Gen. 29:28)

Jacob and Rachel
(Gen. 46:19)

David and Bathsheba
(2 Sam. 12:24)

David—and Michal
(1 Sam. 18:27)

Joseph and Asenath
(Gen. 41:45)

Joseph and Mary (Matt. 1:20)

Who "knew" his wife and she bore a son?

Adam and Eve = Cain (Gen. 4:25)

Jacob and Zilpah = Gad (Gen. 30:10)

Abram and Hagar = Ishmael (Gen. 16:15)

Jacob and Leah = Issachar (Gen. 30:17)

Abraham and Sarai = Isaac (Gen. 21:2)

Boaz and Ruth = Obed (Ruth 4:13)

Jacob and Leah = Reuben (Gen. 29:32)

David and Bathsheba = Solomon (2 Sam. 12:24)

Jacob and Bilhah = Dan (Gen. 30:5)

Hosea and Gomer = Jezreel (Hosea 1:3)

What people wore sackcloth but did not tear their clothes?

Benhadad and his men (1 Kings 20:30–32)

Isaiah (Isa. 20:2)

Eliakim (2 Kings 19:2)

Daniel (Dan. 9:3)

Shebna (2 Kings19:2)

King of Nineveh (Jonah 3:6)

David and the elders (2 Chron. 21:16)

Jews (Esther 4:3)

Job (Job 16:15)

People of Nineveh (Jonah 3:5–6)

What people tore their clothes and wore sackcloth?
Jacob (Gen. 37:34)
Jehoram (2 Kings 6:30)
Joab (2 Sam. 2:31)
Hezekiah (2 Kings 19:1)
Ahab (1 Kings 21:27)
Mordecai (Esther 4:1)

What scribes of the Bible came before Jeremiah's time?
Seraiah (2 Sam. 8:17)
Shemaiah (1 Chron. 24:6)
Sheva (2 Sam. 20:25)
Jeiel (2 Chron. 26:11)
Shebna (2 Kings 18:18)
Shimshai (Ezra 4:8)
Shaphan (2 Kings 22:8)
Ezra (Neh. 8:1)
Shavsha (1 Chron. 18:16)
Zadok (Neh. 13:13)

Who bowed down before men?
Abraham to people of the land (Gen. 23:12)
Mephibosheth to David (2 Sam. 9:8)
Jacob to Esau (Gen. 33:3)
Joab to David (2 Sam. 14:22)
Sisera to Jael (Judges 5:27)
Prophet Nathan to David (1 Kings 1:23)
David to Saul (1 Sam. 24:8)
King Solomon to Bathsheba (1 Kings 2:19)
Saul to Samuel (1 Sam. 28:14)
Amaziah (2 Chron. 25:14)

What groups of people bowed down to someone?

Jacob's wives and children (Gen. 33:6)

Israelites (2 Chron. 7:3)

Brothers of Joseph (Gen. 42:6)

Ezra and the Israelites (Neh. 8:6)

Joseph and 2 children (Gen. 48:12)

Mary Magdalene, Mary mother of Jesus, and others (Luke 24:5)

Who were the monthly captains that served King David?
1 Chronicles 27:1–15

Jashobeam, son of Zabdiel

Ira the son of Ikkesh

Dodai an Ahohite

Helez the Pelonite

Benaiah, son of Jehoiada

Sibbecai the Hushathite

Asahel, brother of Joab

Abiezer the Anetothite

Shamhuth the Izrahite

Maharai the Netophathite

Who were the spies Moses sent to explore the land of Canaan?
Numbers 13: 4–16

Shammua of the tribe of Reuben

Palti of the tribe of Benjamin

Shaphat of the tribe of Simeon

Gaddiel of the tribe of Zebulun

Caleb of the tribe of Judah

Gaddi of the tribe of Joseph/Manasseh

Igal of the tribe of Issachar

Ammiel of the tribe of Dan

Hoshea (Joshua) of the tribe of Ephraim

Sethur of the tribe of Asher

Nahbi from the tribe of Naphtali

Geuel from the tribe of Gad

Who were the rulers of King David's treasures? 1 Chronicles 27:25–31

Azmaveth—king's treasures

Baalhanan—trees in low plains

Jehonathan—storehouses

Joash—oil cellars

Ezri—tillage of the ground

Shitrai—herds in Sharon

Shimei—vineyards

Shaphat—herds in the valleys

Zabdi—wine cellars

Obil—camels

Jaziz—flocks

Who were the princes of Israel's tribes during King David's reign?
1 Chronicles 27:16–22

Eliezer—Reubenites

Omri—Issachar

Shephatiah—Simeonites

Ishmaiah—Zebulun

Elihu—Judah

Jaasiel—Benjamin

Azareel—Dan

Hoshea—Ephraim

Jerimoth—Naphtali

Joel and Iddo—Manasseh

Zadok—Aaronites

Hashabial—Levites

What are the names of two brothers in the Bible?

Jabal and Jubal (Gen. 4:20–21)

Aaron and Moses (Exod. 4:14)

Peleg and Joktan (Gen. 10:25)

Kenaz and Caleb (Joshua 15:17)

Huz and Buz (Gen. 22:21)

Jotham and Abimelech (Judges 9:21)

Jacob and Esau (Gen. 25:26)

Benjamin and Joseph (Gen. 35:24)

Rechad and Baanah (2 Sam. 4:9)

Simon Peter and Andrew (Matt. 4:18)

James and John (Matt. 4:21)

Herod and Philip (Luke 3:1)

What people have fallen asleep in the Old Testament according to the Bible?

Adam (Gen. 2:21)

Joseph (Gen. 41:5)

Noah (Gen. 9:24)

Sesira (Judges 4:21)

Abram (Gen.15:12)

Samson (Judges 16:14)

Jacob (Gen. 28:16)

Samuel (1 Sam. 3:3)

Pharaoh (Gen. 41:4)

Saul (1 Sam. 26:12)

Uriah (2 Sam. 11:9)

Nebuchadnezzar (Dan. 2:1)

Solomon (1 Kings 3:15)

Daniel (Dan. 8:18)

Unnamed mothers
 (1 Kings 3:20)

Jonah (Jonah 1:5)

Elijah (1 Kings 19:5)

Zechariah (Zech. 4:1)

David (Ps. 3:5)

What people have fallen asleep in the New Testament according to the Bible?

Joseph (Matt. 1:24)

Lazarus (John 11:11)

Jesus (Matt. 8:24)

Stephen (Acts 7:60)

12 Virgins (Matt. 25:5)

Prison keeper (Acts 16:27)

Peter and some disciples (Luke 9:32)

Eutychus (Acts 20:9)

What men wept or cried?

Esau (Gen. 27:38)

Jacob (Gen. 27:38)

David (1 Sam. 20:41)

Jonathan (1 Sam. 20:41)

Saul (1 Sam. 24:16)

Joseph (Gen. 43:30)

Joash (2 Kings 13:14)

Benjamin (Gen. 45:14)

Hezekiah (2 Kings 20:3)

Moses (Exod. 2:6)

Jesus (John 11:35)

Peter (Matt. 26:75)

John the Revelator (Rev. 5:4)

Who "cried with a loud voice?"
   Potiphar's wife (Gen. 39:14)
   Witch of Endor (1 Sam. 28:12)
   King David (2 Sam. 19:4)
   Rabshaken/Kings' messengers (2 Kings 18:28)
   Ezekiel (Ezek. 11:13)
   Man with an unclean spirit (Mark 5:7)
   Prosecutors of Stephen (Acts 7:57)
   Stephen (Acts 7:60)
   Paul (Acts 16:28)
   Martyr Saints (Rev. 6:10)

What great men prayed great prayers in the Bible?
   Abraham's prayer for Sodom (Gen. 18:16–33)
   Moses' prayer for Israel in the wilderness (Exod. 32:9–14)
   David's prayer at the end of life (1 Chron. 29:9–20)
   Hezekiah's petitions for deliverance and healing (2 Kings 19:14–19)
   Nehemiah's prayer for success (Neh.1:1–2:9)
   David's prayer for pardon and confession of sin (Ps. 51)
   Daniel's confession on behalf of his people (Dan. 9:1–19)
   Jesus and the Lord's prayer (Matt. 6:5–15)
   Jesus' prayer of submission at Gethsemane (Luke 22:39–46)
   Paul's prayers for the Ephesian believers (Eph. 3:14–21)

Who prayed for victory against the enemy?
   David (2 Sam. 15:31)
   Elisha (2 Kings 6:18)
   Nehemiah (Neh. 4:4–5)
   Isaiah (Isa. 37:20–22)
   Jeremiah (Jer. 12:3)

Who fell down to give honor and worship?

Joseph's brethren (Gen. 50:18)

Cornelius to Peter (Acts 10:25)

Ahimaaz (2 Sam. 18:28)

Three Wise Men (Matt. 2:11)

Shimei (2 Sam. 19:18)

Legion, with unclean spirits (Mark 3:11)

Esther (Esther 8:3)

The sick woman who touched Jesus (Mark 5:33)

People of Babylon (Dan. 3:7)

One of the ten lepers (Luke 17:16)

Servant with large debt (Matt. 18:26, 29)

What people were recorded as having been raised from the dead?

Widow of Zarephath's son (1 Kings 17:22)

Shunammite woman's son (2 Kings 4:34, 35)

Man raised when he came into contact with Elisha's bones (2 Kings 13:20, 21)

Jesus (Matt 28:6; Acts 2:24)

Many holy people in tombs when Jesus gave up his spirit (Matt. 27:52)

Son of Widow from Nain (Luke 7:14, 15)

Jairus' daughter (Luke 8:52–56)

Lazarus (John 11)

Dorcas or Tabitha (Acts 9:40)

Eutychus (Acts 20:9–12)

What people had the title, "Captain of his host?"
Phichol—Abimelech (Gen. 21:22)
Naaman—Syrian king (2 Kings 5:1)
Joshua—God (Joshua 5:14)
Sisera—Jabin's army (Judges 4:7)
Abner—Israel (1 Kings 2:32)
Bidkar—Jehu (2 Kings 9:25)
Amasa—Judah (1 Kings 2:32)
Shophach—Hadarezer (1 Chron. 19:16)
Joab—David (1 Kings 11:21)

What people in the Bible were recorded as raising the dead to life?
Elijah—Widow of Zarephath's son (1 Kings 17:22)
Elisha—Shunammite woman's son (2 Kings 4:34, 35)
Jesus—Lazarus (John 11)
Peter—Dorcas (Acts 9:40)
Paul—Eutychus (Acts 20:9–12)

Who were the widows in the Bible?
Tamar, daughter-in-law of Judah (Gen. 38:11)
Abigail (1 Sam. 25:39)
Zeruah, mother of Jeroboam (1 Kings 11:26)
Bathsheba (2 Sam. 12)
Naomi (Ruth 1:3)
Anna the prophetess (Luke 2:36, 37)
Orpah (Ruth 1:8)
Widow of Zarepath (1 Kings 17:9)
Ruth (Ruth 1:8)
Widow with 2 mites (Mark 12:42)

Who were singers and musicians in the Bible?

Jubal (Gen. 4:21)

Chenaniah (1 Chron. 15:22)

Moses (Exod. 15:1)

Asaph and sons (1 Chron. 25:1)

Henam and sons (1 Chron. 25:1)

Jeduthun and sons (1 Chron. 25:1)

Miriam (Exod. 15:20)

Deborah and Barak (Judges 5:1)

David (2 Sam. 16:23)

Paul and Silas (Acts 16:25)

Who was not a priest but blew a trumpet?

Ehud (Judges 3:27)

Gideon (Judges 6:34)

Sheba (2 Sam. 20:1)

Joab (2 Sam. 20:22)

What people sang in the Bible?

Moses and the Israelites (Exod. 15:1)

Chenaniah (1 Chron. 15:22)

Deborah and Barak (Judges 5:1)

Jezrahiah (Neh. 12:42)

Israelite women (1 Sam. 8:16)

Paul (Acts 16:25)

David and Israel (1 Chron. 13:8)

Silas (Acts 16:25)

What singers were lead by Jezrahiah during Nehemiah's time?
Nehemiah 12:42

Maaseiah
Jehohanan
Shemaiah
Malchijah
Eleazar
Elam
Uzzi
Ezer

What people were mentioned in the Bible who fasted and prayed?
Esther and her attendants (Esther 4:3)
Nehemiah (Neh.1:4)
Mordecai and the Jews (Esther 4:18)
Jehoiakim, son to Josiah (Jer. 36:9)
David (Ps. 35:13)
King Darius (Dan. 6:18)
Jehoshaphat (2 Chron. 20:3)
Daniel (Dan. 9:3)
Ezra and the Israelites (Ezra 8:21)
People of Nineveh (Jonah 3:5)

What people kneeled in prayer?
Solomon (1 Kings 8:54)
Jesus (Luke 22:41)
Ezra (Ezra 9:5)
Stephen (Acts 7:60)
David (Ps. 95:6)
Peter (Acts 9:40)
Daniel (Dan. 9:10)
Paul (Acts 20:36)
Leper asking Jesus for healing (Mark 1:40)
Disciples/People of Tyre (Acts 21:5)

Who called fire down from heaven?

Moses (Exod. 9:23)

Elijah (2 Kings 1:10)

Elisha (2 Kings 6:17)

David (1 Chron. 21:26)

Solomon (2 Chron. 7:1)

Who were the husbands of widows in the Bible?

Er—Tamar (Gen. 38:6)

Nabal—Abigail (1 Sam. 25:3)

Elimelech—Naomi (Ruth 1:2)

Chelion—Orpah (Ruth 1:4)

Mahlon—Ruth (Ruth 1:4)

Uriah—Bathsheba (2 Sam 11:3)

Simeon—Anna (Luke 2:36, 37)

Who were the seven princes of Medo-Persia? Esther 1:14

Carshena

Meres

Shethar

Marsena

Admatha

Memucan

Tarshish

What chamberlains served King Ahasuerus?

Abagtha (Esther 1:10)

Hegai (Esther 2:15)

Bigtha/Biztha (Esther 1:10)

Hege (Esther 2:3)

Bigthana (Esther 6:2)

Mehuman (Esther 1:10)

Carcas (Esther 1:10)

Teresh (Esther 6:2)

Harbona (Esther 1:10)

Shaashgaz (Esther 2:14)

Hatach (Esther 4:5)

Zethar (Esther 1:10)

What Biblical characters committed suicide?

Samson (Judges 16:30)

Ahithophel (2 Sam. 17:23)

King Saul (1 Sam. 31:4)

Saul's armorbearer (1 Sam. 31:5)

Zimri (1 Kings 16:18)

Judas (Matt. 27:3–5)

What people had a personal nurse or caregiver?

Rebekah—Deborah (Gen. 35:8)

Moses—Jochebed (Exod. 2:9)

Obed—Naomi (Ruth 4:16)

Mephibosheth (2 Sam. 4:4)

Joash (2 Kings 11:2)

Who sent out messengers in the Bible?

David (2 Sam. 11:25)

Joab (2 Sam. 11:22)

Jezebel (1 Kings 19:2)

Elisha (2 Kings 5:10)

Paul (Phil. 2:25)

What people received messages from messengers?

Joseph (Gen. 50:16)

Micaiah (1 Kings 22:13)

Samuel (1 Sam. 4:17)

Jehu (2 Kings 9:18)

Saul (1 Sam. 23:27)

Job (Job 1:14)

David (2 Sam. 11:22)

Nebuchadnezzar (Jer. 51:31)

Elijah (1 Kings 19:2)

What people were subjected to fire?
Abednego (Dan. 3:26)
Shadrach (Dan. 3:26)
Meshach (Dan. 3:26)
Abihu (Lev. 10:2)
Nadab (Lev. 10:2)
Complaining Israelites (Num. 11:1)
Samson's wife and her father (Judges 15:6)
Hazor (Joshua 11:11)

What Bible characters had visions, excluding the major prophets?
Abram/Abraham (Gen. 15:1)
Nahum (Nah. 1:1)
Jacob/Israel (Gen. 46:2)
Habakkuk (Hab. 2:2)
Samuel (1 Sam. 3:15)
Ananias (Acts 9:10)
Iddo the seer (2 Chron. 9:29)
Peter (Acts 10:17)
Obadiah (Obad. 1:1)
Paul (Acts 16:9)

What tribes of Israel encamped North and East of the Tabernacle?
Numbers 2

Naphtali
Issachar
Dan
Judah
Asher
Zebulun

What tribes of Israel encamped South and West of the Tabernacle?
Numbers 2

Gad

Manasseh

Reuben

Ephraim

Simeon

Benjamin

Who were the tribal leaders of Israel's twelve tribes? Numbers 2

Judah

Reuben

Ephraim

Dan

What people of the Bible had built friendship with their fellow man?

Abimelech and Ahuzzath (Gen. 26:26)

Job and Zophar (Job 2:11)

Job and Bildad (Job 2:11)

Job and Eliphaz (Job 2:11)

Judah and Hirah (Gen. 38:12)

Amnon and Jonadab (2 Sam. 13:3)

David and Hushai (2 Sam. 15:37)

Pilate and Ceasar (John 19:12)

Pilate and Herod (Luke 23:12)

Blastus and Tyre and Sidon (Acts 12:20)

What people hosted or attended a party?

    Joseph fed his brethren (Gen. 43:16–34)

    Sons of David (2 Sam. 13:23–39)

    Pharaoh's birthday (Gen. 40:20)

    Jesus at the wedding in Cana (John 2:1–11)

    Queen Esther called for the king and Haman (Esther 7:1–6)

    Disciples the night before Passover (Matt. 26:17–30)

    King Darius the night of the writing on the wall (Dan. 5)

    The Prodigal Son (Luke 15:22–32)

    Children of Job (Job 1:13)

    Herodias at Herod's birthday (Matt. 14:6)

What people got sick of leprosy?

    Moses (Exod. 4:6)

    Miriam (Num. 12:10)

    Naaman (2 Kings 5:27)

    Gehazi and Kin (2 Kings 5:27)

    Uzziah (2 Chron. 26:19)

What people fled and sought refuge in Egypt?

    Abram and family (Gen. 12:10)

    People of Judah and army commanders (2 Kings 25:26)

    Jacob and family (Gen. 46:6)

    Urijah (Jer. 26:21)

    Hadad the Edomite (1 Kings 11:17)

    Jeremiah (Jer. 43:6, 7)

    Jeroboam (1 Kings 11:40)

    Mary and Joseph with Baby Jesus (Matt. 2:13)

What Old Testament Bible men "ran" or fled?

Abraham (Gen. 18:7)

Samuel (1 Sam. 3:5)

Laban (Gen. 24:29)

David (1 Sam. 17:51)

Esau (Gen. 33:4)

Ahimaaz (2 Sam. 18:23)

Joseph (Gen. 39:12)

Elijah/Elisha (1 Kings 19:3, 20)

Aaron (Num. 16:47)

Gehazi (2 Kings 5:21)

What New Testament Bible men "ran?"

The Prodigal Son's father (Luke 15:17–24)

Philip (Acts 8:30)

Zaccheus (Luke 19:4)

Barnabas (Acts 14:14)

Paul (Acts 14:14)

Peter (Luke 24:12)

John and other disciples (John 20:4)

What men were called and replied, "here I am?"

Isaac/Abraham (Gen. 22:7)

Joseph/Jacob (Gen. 37:13)

Esau/Isaac (Gen. 27:1)

Samuel/Eli (1 Sam. 3:16)

Jacob/Isaac (Gen. 27:18)

Ahitub/Saul (1 Sam. 22:12)

Who was compared to a "dog?"
Philistine "Goliath" (1 Sam. 17:43)
Hazael (2 Kings 8:13)
David (1 Sam. 24:14)
Evil men (Ps. 22:16)
Mephibosheth, the son of Jonathan (2 Sam. 9:8)
Abishai (2 Sam. 16:9)
Syro-Phoenician woman (Mark 7:27)
Wicked men (Phil. 3:2)

Who preached and called for repentance saying, "repent ye?"
Jeremiah (Jer. 25:5)
Disciples (Mark 6:12)
Ezekiel (Ezek. 14:6)
Peter (Acts 2:38)
John the Baptist (Matt. 3:1, 2)
Paul (Acts 26:20)
Jonah (Matt. 12:41; Luke 11:32)
John (Rev. 2:22)
Jesus (Mark 1:14, 15; Matt. 4:7)

Nehemiah listed what exiles who returned to Jerusalem? Nehemiah 7:6–7
Zerubbabel and Joshua
Bilshan
Nehemiah and Azariah
Mispereth
Raamiah
Bigvai
Nahamani
Nehum
Mordecai
Baanah

What kings or leaders did things at night?
Abram to save his captured brother (Gen. 14:15)
Pharaoh knowing his first born died (Exod. 12:30)
Joshua sent armies to Ai (Joshua 8:3)
Gideon broke down the altar of Baal (Judges 6:27)
Samuel inquired of the Lord regarding King Saul (1 Sam. 15:16)
David fled and escaped from King Saul (1 Sam. 19:10)
King Saul sleeping in the cave when David found him (1 Sam 26:7)
King Saul disguised himself and visited the woman of Endor
   (1 Sam 28:8)

Who went to battle and fought at night?
Joshua battled with the King of Ai (Joshua 8:13)
Gideon battled with Midianites and Amalikites (Judges 7:8–11)
Saul battled with the Philistines (1 Sam. 14:36)
Joram battled with the Edomites (2 Kings 8:21)
Angel of the Lord smote the Assyrians (2 Kings 19:35)
Jehoram smote the Edomites (2 Chron. 21:9)

What people lived in the wilderness of Paran?
Hagar (Gen. 21:21)
Ishmael (Gen. 21:21)
Aaron (Num. 13:26)
David (1 Sam.25:1)
Miriam (Num. 12:15–16)
Hadad (1 Kings 11:17–19)
Moses (Num. 13:3)
Children of Israel (Num. 10:11–13)

What people in the Bible are described as "goodly?"

Joseph—goodly person (Gen. 39:6)

David—goodly to look at (1 Sam. 16:12)

Moses—goodly child (Exod. 2:2)

Adonijah—goodly man (1 Kings 1:6)

Saul—goodly (1 Sam. 9:2)

Egyptian—goodly man (2 Sam. 23:21)

Who were the "valiant" men in the Bible?

David (1 Sam. 18:17)

Rephaiah (1 Kings 1:42)

Abner (1 Sam. 26:15)

Jeriel (1 Kings 1:42)

Benaiah (2 Sam. 23:20)

Jahmai (1 Kings 1:42)

Jonathan the son of Abiathar (1 Kings 1:42)

Jibsam (1 Kings 1:42)

Tola (1 Kings 1:42)

Shemuel (1 Chron. 7:2)

Who was a "Mighty Man of Valour?"

Gideon (Judges 6:12)

Sons of Ulam (1 Chron. 8:40)

Jephthah (Judges 11:1)

Zadok (1 Chron. 12:28)

Jeroboam (1 Kings 11:28)

Eliada (2 Chron. 17:17)

Naaman (2 Kings 5:1)

Who were governors in the Old Testament?

Joseph—Egypt (Gen. 45:26)

Obadiah—house of King Ahab (1 Kings 18:3)

Amon—Samaria during King Ahab (1 Kings 22:26)

Joshua—during reign of King Josiah of Judah (2 Kings 23:8)

Gedaliah—Judah appointed by Nebuchadnezzar (2 Kings 25:23)

Maaseiah—during reign of King Josiah (2 Chron. 34:8)

Tatnai—during reign of King Darius (Ezra 5:6)

Sheshbazzar—during reign of King Cyrus (Ezra 5:14)

Nehemiah—Judah during reign of King Artaxerxes (Neh. 5:14)

Zerubbabel—Judah during reign of King Darius (Hag. 1:1)

Who took off their sandals?

Moses (Exod. 3:5)

Close relative of Boaz (Ruth 4:7)

Brother's wife (Deut. 25:9)

Isaiah (Isa. 20:2)

Joshua (Joshua 5:15)

Peter (Acts 12:8)

What man was riding in a chariot?

Joseph (Gen. 46:29)

Ahab (1 Kings 18:44, 45)

Pharaoh (Exod. 14:9)

Elijah (2 Kings 2:11)

Adonijah (1 Kings 1:5)

Naaman (2 Kings 5:9)

King Rehoboam (1 Kings 12:18)

Jehu (2 Kings 9:16)

Zimri (1 Kings 16:9)

Absalom (2 Sam. 15:1)

Ahaziah the king of Judah (2 Kings 9:27)

Who are the different Josephs in the Bible?

Joseph—son of Jacob and Rachel (Gen. 37:3)

Joseph—son of Igal, from the tribe of Issachar (Num. 13:7)

Joseph—son of Asaph, musician during King David (1 Chron. 25:9)

Joseph—priest, son of Bani (Ezra 10:42)

Joseph—priest in the days of Joiakim (Neh. 12:12, 14)

Joseph—father of Jesus (Matt. 1:18–25)

Joseph—great-grandfather of Jesus (Luke 3:23–38)

Joseph of Arimathaea (John 19:38–42)

Joseph Justus—also called Barsabas (Acts 1:23)

Who are the different Simons of the Bible?

Simon, brother of Jesus (Matt. 13:55)

Simon the father of Judas Iscariot (John 6:71)

Simon the Canaanite/Zealot (Matt. 10:4)

Simon Peter (John 6:68)

Simon from Cyrene (Mark 15:21)

Simon the sorcerer/magician (Acts 8:9)

Simon the leper (Mark 14:3)

Simon the tanner (Acts 9:43)

Simon the Pharisee (Luke 7:40)

Who rent or tore their clothes?

Reuben (Gen. 37:29)

King Ahab (1 Kings 21:27)

King of Israel (2 Kings 5:7, 8)

Tamar (2 Sam. 13:19)

Jacob (Gen. 37:34)

Elisha (2 Kings 2:12)

King of Judah (2 Kings 22:19)

Mordecai (Esther 4:1)

Joseph's brethren (Gen. 44:13)

Athaliah (2 Kings 11:14)

A man of Benjamin
(1 Sam. 4:12)

Caiaphas the high priest
(Matt. 26:65)

Joshua (Joshua 7:6)

Hezekiah (2 Kings 18:37)

David and his men (2 Sam. 1:11)

Paul and Barnabas (Acts 14:14)

Jephthah (Judges 11:35)

Josiah (2 Kings 22:11)

Amalikite soldier (2 Sam. 1:2)

Magistrates (Acts 16:22)

Who "rose up early in the morning?"

Abraham (Gen. 21:14)

Joshua (Joshua 6:12)

Abraham's servant (Gen. 24:54)

David (1 Sam. 29:11)

Isaac (Gen. 26:31)

Samuel (1 Sam. 15:12)

Jacob (Gen. 28:18)

David (1 Sam. 17:20)

Laban (Gen. 31:55)

Job (Job 1:5)

Moses (Exod. 34:4)

Children of Israel
(Judges 20:19)

Abimelech (Judges 9:33)

Balaam (Num. 22:21)

Hannah and Elkanah
(1 Sam. 1:19)

Visiting Levite man
(Judges 19:27)

Moabites (2 Kings 3:22)

Who did Nebuchadnezzar take captive to Babylon from Judah?
2 Kings 24:15, 16

King Jehoiachin

King's officers

King's mother

All mighty men of valour

King's princes

All craftsmen and smiths

King's servants

Who were princes of King Nebuchadnezzar of Babylon? Jeremiah 39:3

Rabsaris

Samgarnebo

Nergalsharezer

Sarsechim

Rabmag

What was found on both the right hand and left hand?

Red Sea wall of water (Exod. 14:29)

Pillars of Samson (Judges 16:29)

The host of Heaven on the right and left side of the Lord (1 Kings 22:19)

Zebedee's sons (James and John) (Matt. 20:21)

Who had to make a choice to go right or go left?

Lot and Abram (Gen. 13:9)

Solomon (2 Chron. 34:2)

Abraham's servant to Laban and Bethuel (Gen. 24:49)

Wise woman of Tekoah (2 Sam. 14:19)

Moses and the Israelites (Num. 20:17)

Ninevites (Jonah 4:11)

Balaam and the donkey (Num. 22:26)

Ezekiel (Ezek. 21:16)

Joshua (Joshua 23:6)

Who was mentioned in the Bible as "cunning" or skillful?

Esau (Gen. 25:27)

Hiram (1 Kings 7:13–15)

Bezaleel the son of Uri (Exod. 31:1–4)

Asaph (1 Chron. 25:6–8)

Aholiab, the son of Ahisamach (Exod. 35:33–35)

Jeduthun (1 Chron. 25:6–8)

David (1 Sam. 16:16, 18, 23)

Heman (1 Chron. 25:6–8)

What people owned an instrument or things made of iron?
>   Og, king of Bashan—Bed-stead (Deut. 3:11)
>   Ahab—Horn (1 Kings 22:11)
>   Canaanites—Chariots (Joshua 17:16)
>   Sisera—Chariots (Judges 4:13)
>   Goliath—Spear's head (1 Sam. 17:7)
>   David—Nails (1 Chron. 22:3)

Who offered one spoon of gold and one silver bowl for the dedication of the altar?
>   Nahshon, son of Amminadab, prince of Judah (Num. 7:12–17)
>   Nethaneel, son of Zuar, prince of Issachar (Num. 7:18–23)
>   Eliab, son of Helon, prince of Zebulun (Num. 7:24–29)
>   Elizur, son of Shedeur, prince of Reuben (Num. 7:30–35)
>   Shelumiel, son of Zurishaddai, prince of Simeon (Num. 7:36–41)
>   Eliasaph, son of Deuel, prince of Gad (Num. 7:42–27)
>   Elishama, son of Ammihud, prince of Ephraim (Num 7:48–53)
>   Gamaliel, son of Pedahzur, prince of Manasseh (Num. 7:54–59)
>   Abidan, son of Gideoni, prince of Benjamin (Num. 7:60–65)
>   Ahiezer, son of Ammishaddai, prince of Dan (Num. 7:66–71)
>   Pagiel, son of Ocran, prince of Asher (Num. 7:72–77)
>   Ahira, son of Enan, prince of Naphtali (Num. 7:78–83)

What people hid themselves in a cave?
>   Adoni-Zedek, king of Jerusalem (Joshua 10:3, 16)
>   Hoham, king of Hebron (Joshua 10:3, 16)
>   Piram, king of Jarmuth (Joshua 10:3, 16)
>   Japhia, king of Lachish (Joshua 10:3, 16)
>   Debir, king of Eglon (Joshua 10:3, 16)
>   Prophets (1 Kings 18:4)
>   Elijah (1 Kings 19:9)
>   Saul's army (1 Sam. 13:6)
>   David (1 Sam. 22:1)
>   King Saul (1 Sam. 24:3)

Who hid herself/himself or was hidden?

Adam (Gen. 3:8)

Eve (Gen. 3:8)

David (1 Sam. 20:24)

Elijah the Tishbite (1 Kings 17:3)

Moses (Exod. 2:2)

Joash (2 Kings 11:2, 3)

Jotham (Judges 9:5)

Elisabeth (Luke 1:24)

Saul (1 Sam. 10:22)

Jesus (John 12:36)

2 spies or messengers (Joshua 2:6)

4 sons of Ornan (1 Chron. 21:20)

What Bible characters hid something?

Rachel—Idols (Gen. 31:34)

Mother—son from being eaten (2 Kings 6:29)

Jacob—strange gods and earrings (Gen. 35:4)

Lepers—silver, gold, raiment (2 Kings 7:8)

Israel—sin through ignorance (Lev. 4:13)

David—God's word (Ps. 119:11)

Achan—spoils from war (Joshua 7:20–21)

Jeremiah—Linen girdle, stone (Jer. 13:5; 43:9)

Gideon—wheat (Judges 6:11)

What people in the Bible were recorded buying land?

Jacob (Gen. 33:19; Joshua 24:32)

Omri (1 Kings 16:24)

Joseph (Gen. 47:20)

Jeremiah (Jer. 32:9)

Abraham (Gen. 49:30)

Chief priest (Matt. 27:5–7)

David (2 Sam. 24:24)

Judas (Acts 1:16–18)

What people sold parcels of land?

Hamor to Jacob (Gen. 33:19)

Shemer to Omri (1 Kings 16:24)

Egyptians to Joseph (Gen. 47:20)

Ornan the Jebusite (1 Chron. 21:18–25)

Ephron the Hittite to Abraham (Gen. 49:30)

Hanameel to Jeremiah (Jer. 32:9)

Who made a purchase other than land?

Abraham—servant (Gen. 17:23)

Hosea—Gomer (Hosea 3:2)

Midianites/Ishmaelites—Joseph (Gen. 37:28)

Joseph of Arimathaea—Fine linen (Mark 15:46)

Potiphar—Joseph (Gen. 39:1)

Mary Magdalene, Mary mother of James, Salome—Sweet spices (Mark 16:1)

Joseph's brethren and others—corn (Gen. 47:14)

David—Oxen (2 Sam. 24:24)

God—You (1 Cor. 6:20)

What people owned silver and gold?

Abram (Gen. 13:2)

David (2 Sam. 8:11)

Isaac (Gen. 24:35)

Solomon (1 Kings 15:15)

Rebekah (Gen. 24:53)

Benhadad (1 Kings 15:18)

Balak (Num. 22:18)

Hezekiah (2 Chron. 32:27)

Achan (Joshua 7:21, 24)

Who were David's officials in the kingdom? 1 Chronicles 18:14–17, 2 Samuel 20:24, 26

Joab, son of Zeruah—army commander in chief

Behaiah, son of Jehoida—commander of David's bodyguard

Jehoshaphat, son Alihud—keeper of government records

David's sons were his high-ranking officials

Zadok, son of Ahitub—priest

Adoram—in-charge of slave labor force

Ahimelech, son of Abiathar—priest

Ira—chief ruler

Shavsha/Sheva—secretary

Who cast earth, dust, or ashes on their head?

Children of Israel (Neh. 9:1)

Tamar (2 Sam. 13:19)

Joshua and Elders of Israel (Joshua 7:6)

Job and his friends (Job 2:12)

Man of Benjamin (1 Sam. 4:12)

Elders of the daughters of Zion (Lam. 2:10)

Amalikite man reporting to David (2 Sam. 1:2)

Merchants of the earth (Rev.18:19)

Hushai the Archite (2 Sam. 15:32)

Who were Ethiopians (Cushite) in the Bible?

Moses' 2nd wife (Num. 12:1)

Zerah (2 Chron. 14:9)

Ebedmelech (Jer. 38:7)

Ethiopian Eunuch (Peter baptized) (Acts 8:27)

Queen Candace (Acts 8:27)

Who were Syrians in the Bible?
Rebekah (Gen. 25:20)
Bethuel (Gen. 25:20)
Laban (Gen. 25:20)
Hazael, king of Syria (2 Kings 8:28)
Rezin, king of Syria (2 Kings 16:6)
Shophach, captain of the host (1 Chron. 19:16)
Naaman (2 Kings 5:20)

Who in the Bible had wine?
Melchizedek, king of Salem (Gen. 14:18)
Jesse (1 Sam. 16:20)
Abigail (1 Sam. 25:18)
Isaac (Gen. 27:37)
Ziba the servant of Mephibosheth (2 Sam. 16:1)
Judah (Gen. 49:11)
King Artaxerxes (Neh. 2:1)
Hannah (1 Sam. 1:24)
Esther (Esther 7:2)

Bible character were recorded as drinking wine?
Noah (Gen. 9:21, 24)
Amnon (2 Sam. 13:28)
Lot (Gen. 19:32, 34)
King Ahasuerus (Esther 1:10)
Isaac (Gen. 27:25)
Job's sons and daughters (Job 1:13)
Nazarite (Num. 6:20)
Belshazzar (Dan. 5:1)
Nabal (1 Sam. 25:37)
Nebuchadnezzar (Dan. 5:2)

Who were Paul's relatives?

Andronicus (Romans 16:7)

Junia (Romans 16:7)

Herodion (Romans 16:11)

Rufus (Romans 16:13)

Marcus (1 Peter 5:13)

What people are associated with Paul's capture?

Claudius Lysias, the chief captain (Acts 21:31–33, 23:26)

Porcius Festus, who replaced Felix as governor (Acts 24:27)

Ananias, the high priest (Acts 23:1–2)

King Agrippa and his wife, Bernice (Acts 25:13,23)

Felix, the governor, and wife Drusilla (Acts 23:23–24)

Caesar Augustus, Roman king (Acts 25:21, Luke 2:1)

Tertullus, orator (Acts 24:1)

Julius, a centurion (Acts 27:1)

What people were anointed?

Aaron by Moses (Lev. 8:30)

Nadab, son of Aaron, by Moses (Lev. 8:30)

Abihu, son of Aaron, by Moses (Lev. 8:30)

Eleazar, son of Aaron, by Moses (Lev. 8:30)

Ithamar, son of Aaron, by Moses, (Lev. 8:30)

Solomon by Zadok and Nathan (1 Kings 1:34)

Hazael by Elijah (1 Kings 19:15–16)

Elisha by Elijah (1 Kings 19:15–16)

Jehu by Elijah/Elisha (1 Kings 19:15–16)

Joash by Jehoiada (2 Kings 11:12)

Saul by Samuel (1 Sam. 10:1)

David by Samuel (1 Sam. 16:13)

Jesus by Mary (John 11:2, 3)

What people begat children in their 30's?

Reu—Serug (thirty-two years old) (Gen. 11:20)

Salah—Eber (thirty years old) (Gen. 11:14)

Eber—Peleg (thirty-four years old) (Gen. 11:16)

Peleg—Reu (thirty years old) (Gen. 11:18)

Arphaxad—Salah (thirty-five years old) (Gen. 11:12)

Serug—Nahor (thirty years old) (Gen. 11:22)

What people were more than 100 years old at the birth of their children?

Shem—Arphaxad (100 years old) (Gen. 11:10)

Jared—Enoch (162 years old) (Gen. 5:18)

Abraham—Isaac (100 years old) (Gen. 21:5)

Lamech—Noah (182 years old) (Gen. 5:28–29)

Seth—Enos (105 years old) (Gen. 5:6)

Methuselah—Lamech (187 years old) (Gen. 5:25)

Adam—Seth (138 years old) (Gen. 5:3)

Noah—Shem (500 years old) (Gen. 5:21)

Who were Benjamites mentioned in the Bible?

Palti, spy to Canaan (Num. 13:9)

Aphiah (1 Sam. 9:1)

Ehud, son of Gera, a left-handed deliverer (Judges 3:15)

Abishai who cursed David (2 Sam. 16:11)

Kish, a mighty man of power (1 Sam. 9:1)

Shimei, son of Gera (2 Sam. 19:16)

Abiel (1 Sam. 9:1)

Sheba, son of Bichri, blew trumpet (2 Sam. 20:1)

Zeror (1 Sam. 9:1)

Abiezer the Anetothite (1 Chron. 27:12)

Bechorath (1 Sam. 9:1)

Mordecai, son of Jair (Esther 2:5)

Who in the Bible cursed someone?

Isaac said to Jacob, "cursed be everyone that curseth thee" (Gen. 27:29)

Jacob said to his sons Simeon and Levi, "cursed be their anger" (Gen. 49:7)

Joshua saying, "cursed be the man before the Lord" (Joshua 6:26)

Saul saying, "cursed be the man that eateth any food until evening" (1 Sam. 14:24)

Philistine cursed David by his gods (1 Sam. 17:43)

Elisha cursed the children that mocked him (2 Kings 2:22–24)

Whose birth was foretold or announced?

Ishmael (Gen. 16:11)

Josiah (1 Kings 13:2)

Isaac (Gen. 21:1–5)

Shunammite's son (2 Kings 4:12–17)

Samson (Judges 13:2–5)

John the Baptist (Luke 1:13)

Samuel (1 Sam. 1:17–22)

Jesus (Luke 1:30–31)

Whose death was foretold?

Pharaoh's baker (Gen. 40:19)

Hezekiah (2 Kings 20:1–6)

Moses (Deut. 31:14)

Hananiah (Jer. 28:15–17)

Saul (1 Sam. 28:19, 20)

Messiah-Jesus (Dan. 9:26)

Ahaziah (2 Kings 1:2, 4)

Who was deceived and who deceived them?
Eve was deceived by Satan (1 Tim. 2:14)
Israelite midwives deceived Pharaoh (Exod. 1:17–19)
Abraham deceived Abimelech (Gen. 20:1–3)
Samuel deceived Saul to anoint David (1 Sam. 16:1–3)
Isaac deceived Abimelech (Gen. 26:6–10)
Michal deceived her father, Saul (1 Sam. 19:15–17)
Jacob deceived his father, Isaac (Gen. 27:19–20)
Saul disguised himself to see woman of Endor (1 Sam. 28:8–12)
Laban had deceived Jacob (Gen. 31:7)
Delilah deceived Samson (Judges 16)

Who was mentioned as a father-in-law?
Judah to Tamar (Gen. 38:13)
Jethro to Moses (Exod. 3:1)
Hobab to Moses (Judges 4:11)
Eli to Phinehas (1 Sam. 4:19)
Annas to Caiaphas (John 18:13)

Who died by hanging?
Chief Baker (Gen. 40:22)
Saul (2 Sam. 21:12–13)
Jonathan (2 Sam. 21:12–13)
Ishbosheth (2 Sam. 4:12)
Ahithophel (2 Sam. 17:23)
Haman (Esther 8:7)
Armoni (2 Sam. 21:6–9)
Haman's ten sons (Esther 9:13–14)
Mephibosheth (2 Sam. 21:6–9)
Five sons of Michal (2 Sam. 21:6–9)
Judas (Matt. 27:5)

Who did the Lord kill or smite in extraordinary ways?

Egyptians—Hail storm (Exod. 9:25)

Firstborn in Egypt—Passover (Gen. 12:29)

Complaining Israelites (Num. 11:1–3)

Amorites—stones from heaven (Joshua 10:10–11)

Men of Beth-shemesh who looked into the Ark of the LORD (1 Sam. 6:19)

Israelites—sent pestilence (2 Sam. 24:14–17)

"The anger of the Lord" was kindled against whom?

Moses (Exod. 4:14)

Jeroboam (1 Kings 15:30)

Aaron (Num. 12:6–9)

Baasha and Elah his son (1 Kings 16:13)

Miriam (Num. 12:6–9)

Ahab (1 Kings 16:33)

Balaam (Num. 22:22)

Judah (2 Kings 23:26)

Israel (Num. 25:3)

Amaziah (2 Chron. 28:25)

Uzzah (2 Sam. 6:7)

Who has or used a spear to kill?

Joshua (Joshua 8:18)

Lahmi, brother Goliath (2 Sam. 21:19)

Goliath (1 Sam. 17:5–7)

Adino (2 Sam. 23:8)

Saul (1 Sam. 26:7)

Abishai (2 Sam. 23:18)

Abner (2 Sam. 2:23)

Benaiah (2 Sam. 23:20–21)

Ishbibenob (2 Sam. 21:16)

Jashobeam (1 Chron. 11:11)

Soldier, pierced Jesus (John 19:34)

What seven Jewish men from Antioch were chosen for a special work by the Apostles? Acts 6:2–5

Stephen

Timon

Philip

Parmenas

Prochorus

Nicolaus

Nicanor

What people laid hands on others?

Israel/Jacob (Gen. 48:14)

John (Acts 8:17)

Moses (Num. 27:22–23)

Ananias (Acts 9:17)

Jesus (Luke 4:40)

Church members of Antioch (Acts 13:1–3)

Apostles (Acts 6:5–6)

Paul (Acts 19:6–7)

Peter (Acts 8:17)

What people had hands laid upon him?

Ephraim (Gen. 48:14)

Manasseh (Gen. 48:14)

Men of Samaria (Acts 8:17)

Saul/Paul (Acts 9:17)

Joshua (Num. 27:22–23)

Barnabas (Acts 13:1–3)

David (Ps. 139:5)

Saul (Acts 13:1–3)

Sick men and women (Luke 4:40)

Father of Publius (Acts 28:8)

Who had an encounter with a lion?

Samson (Judges 14:5–9)

Neighbour of a prophet (1 Kings 20:35–36)

David (1 Sam. 17:34–37)

People from Assyrian kingdom placed in Samaria (2 Kings 17:23–26)

Benaiah (2 Sam. 23:20)

Daniel (Dan. 6:20–24)

Disobedient man of God (1 Kings 13:24–26)

Paul (2 Tim. 4:17)

What people dwelled or lived in a tent?

Adah and Jabal (Gen. 4:20)

Isaac (Gen. 26:17)

Noah (Gen. 9:20–21)

Leah and Rachel (Gen. 31:33)

Abram (Gen. 12:7–8)

Jethro (Exod. 18:7)

Lot (Gen. 13:5)

Achan (Joshua 7:20–21)

Jacob (Gen. 25:27)

Heber (Judges 4:11)

Who saw lightning or heard thunder?

Moses (Exod. 9:23)

Samuel (1 Sam. 12:17–18)

Pharaoh (Exod. 9:33–34)

Job (Job 38:35)

Israelites (Exod. 20:18)

John the Revelator (Rev. 8:5)

Philistines (1 Sam. 7:10)

Who was married to a relative?

Abraham's wife Sarah was his half sister (Gen. 20:11–12)

Isaac married his second cousin Rebekah (Gen. 24:4, 15)

Jacob married his cousin Leah (Gen. 29:21–23)

Jacob married his cousin Rachel (Gen. 29:28–30)

Amram married his aunt (Exod. 6:20)

Mahlah married daughters of Zelophehad, his cousins (Num. 36:11)

Tirzah married daughters of Zelophehad, his cousins (Num. 36:11)

Hoglah married daughters of Zelophehad, his cousins (Num. 36:11)

Milcah married daughters of Zelophehad, his cousins (Num. 36:11)

Noah married daughters of Zelophehad, his cousins (Num. 36:11)

What married men of the Bible had an unnamed wife?

Cain (Gen. 4:17)

Abiram (Num. 16:27)

Noah (Gen. 7:7)

Gideon (Judges 8:30)

Lot (Gen. 19:15)

Manoah (Judges 13:2)

Potiphar's wife (Gen. 39:7–12)

Phinehas (1 Sam. 4:19)

Dathan (Num. 16:27)

Samuel (1 Sam. 18:1)

Hadad (1 Kings 11:19–20)

Abijah (2 Chron. 13:21)

Naaman (2 Kings 5:2)

Job (Job 2:9)

Jarha (2 Chron. 2:35)

Ezekiel (Ezek. 24:15–18)

Ephraim (2 Chron. 7:22–23)

Peter (Matt. 8:14)

What men took "strange" or pagan wives according to the Bible?

Gilead (Judges 11:2)

Eliezer (Ezra 10:18)

Shechaniah (Ezra 10:2)

Jarib (Ezra 10:18)

Maaseiah (Ezra 10:18)

Gedaliah (Ezra 10:18)

What men are mentioned as writing a letter?
David (2 Sam. 11:14)
Rehum (Ezra 4:9)
Jehu (2 Kings 10:1)
Haman (Esther 8:5)
Shemaiah (1 Chron. 24:6)
Mordecai (Esther 9:20)
Hezekiah (2 Chron. 30:1)
King Darius (Dan. 6:25)
Shimshai (Ezra 4:8)
Pilate (John 19:19)

What men are mentioned in the Bible as having no sons or children?
Nadab and Abihu (Num. 3:4)
Ahaziah (2 Kings 1:17–18)
Zelophehad (Num. 26:3)
Sheshan (1 Chron. 2:34)
Absalom (2 Sam. 18:18)
Eleazar (1 Chron. 23:22)

What men went to a mountain?
Abraham—Mt. Moriah (Gen. 22:1–2)
Isaac—Mt. Moriah (Gen. 22:1–2)
Ahab—Mt. Carmel (1 Kings 18:42–45)
Elijah—Mt. Horeb (1 Kings 19:8–10)
Moses—Mt. Horeb (Exod. 3:1–2)
Moses—Mt. Sinai (Exod. 19:1–3)
Elijah—Mt. Carmel (1 Kings 18:42–45)
John—Mt. of Transfiguration (Hermon) (Matt. 17:1–3)
Peter—Mt. of Transfiguration (Hermon) (Matt. 17:1–3)
James—Mt. of Transfiguration (Hermon) (Matt. 17:1–3)

Who requested to be killed?
Moses (Num. 11:15)
Abimelech (Judges 9:53–54)
Saul (1 Sam. 31:4)
Elijah (1 Kings 19:4)
Jonah (Jonah 4:3)

What men are mentioned as having a son-in-law?
Lot (Gen. 19:12)
Ahab—Ahaziah (2 Kings 8:27)
Timnite—Samson (Judges 15:6)
Shechaniah—Tobiah (Neh. 6:17–19)
Saul—David (1 Sam. 18:18)
Sanballat—Benaiah (Neh. 13:28)

What Bible are characters are referenced when the Bible talks about a son and a son's son?
Terah (Gen. 11:31)
Israel (Deut. 6:1–3)
Abimelech (Gen. 21:22–23)
Gideon (Judges 8:22)
Jacob (Gen. 46:5–7)
Job (Job 42:16)
Moses (Exod. 10:1–2)
Nebuchadnezzar (Jer. 27:6–7)

What Bible characters experienced a storm?
Noah (Gen. 6)
Jonah (Jonah 1:3–4)
Wise man who built upon a rock (Matt. 7:24–25)
Jesus (Matt. 8:23–27)
Paul (Acts 27:1–2)

Who did something for three days and three nights?

Egyptians—did not eat (1 Sam. 30:11–12)

Modecai and the Jews—Fasting (Esther 4:16)

Esther and her maids—Fasting (Esther 4:16)

Jonah—in the belly of fish (Jonah 1:17)

Son of man (Jesus)—in the heart of the earth (Matt. 12:40)

What Old Testament Bible characters had significant events happen in a three-day period of their lives?

Pharaoh's butler restored to service after three days (Gen. 40:13)

Pharaoh's baker hung on a tree after three days (Gen. 40:18)

Joseph put all his brothers in prison for three days (Gen. 42:17)

Philistines had not come up with an answer to Samson's riddle after three days (Judges 14:14)

Saul looked for his father's donkey (1 Sam. 9:20)

David and soldiers in a mission asked for bread at the temple (1 Sam. 21:5)

Jonathan met David at the meeting place (1 Sam. 20:19)

Elisha sent fifty men to look for three days and could not find Elijah (2 Kings 2:17)

Jehoshaphat's troops gathered the spoils from the Moabites and Ammonites (2 Chron. 20:25)

Jonah went unto Nineveh in three days journey (Jonah 3:3)

What New Testament Bible characters had significant events happen in a three-day period of their lives?

Son of man—three days in the "heart of the earth" (Matt. 12:40)

Multitude—with Jesus three days (Matt. 15:32)

Son of God—build the temple in three days (Matt. 26:61)

Mary and Joseph came back after three days journey and found Jesus at the temple (Luke 2:46)

Paul landing at Syracuse and tarried there three days (Acts 28:12)

Who should not drink strong drink according to the Bible?

Aaron and his sons (Lev. 10:9)

Samson (Judges 13:14)

Nazarite (Num. 6:3)

Hannah (1 Sam. 1:15)

Manoah's wife (Judges 13:14)

John the Baptist (Luke 1:15)

Who made an oath to his fellow man?

God to Abraham (Gen. 26:3)

King Saul with the people (1 Sam. 14:28)

Isaac and Abibelech (Gen. 26:29)

David and Jonathan (1 Sam. 21:7)

Joseph and children of Israel (Gen. 50:25)

Paul (Acts 18:18)

Who was recorded in the Bible being seen "eating and drinking?"

Boaz after harvest (Ruth 3:3)

Amalekites after plundering Philistines (1 Sam. 30:16)

People in Judah and Israel during Solomon's reign (1 Kings 4:20)

Israelites who came to Hebron to make David king (1 Chron. 12:39)

Children of Job (Job 1:13)

Men of Judah in Isaiah's time (Isa. 22:13)

The Son of man (Matt. 11:19)

People before Noah's flood (Matt. 24:38)

Seventy-plus disciples that God sent in pairs to all the towns and villages (Luke 10:7)

Of what nationality were Solomon's wives? 1 Kings 11:1

Egyptian, Daughter of Pharaoh

Edomites

Moabites

Zidonians

Ammonites

Hitites

David had wars with and scored victories over whom?

Philistines (2 Sam. 8:1)

Edomites (1 Chron. 18:13)

Moabites (2 Sam. 8:2)

Ammonites (2 Sam. 10:11, 12)

King Hadadezer in Hamath (2 Sam. 8:3; 10:15, 16)

Amalekites (2 Sam. 8:12)

Syrians of Damascus, Beth-Rehob (2 Sam. 8:5, 6)

Syrian kingdoms of Maacah and Zobah (1 Chron. 19:7)

Tol, King of Hamath (2 Sam. 8: 9, 10)

King Saul fought wars against what Israelite enemies?

Moabites (1 Sam. 14:47)

King of Zobah (1 Sam. 14:47)

Ammonites (1 Sam. 14:47)

Philistines (1 Sam. 14:47)

Edomites (1 Sam. 14:47)

Amalekites (1 Sam. 14:48)

What groups of people used chariots in war?

Egyptians (Exod. 14:7)

Canaanites (Joshua 17:16)

Israelites (Judges 4:3)

Philistines (1 Sam. 13:5)

Syrians (1 Sam. 10:18)

Assyrians (2 Kings 19:23)

Ethiopians (2 Chron. 14:9)

Babylonians (Ezekiel 26:7)

What groups of people did Israel not drive out of the promised land?

Gibeonites (Joshua 9:2–5)

Canaanites (Joshua 17:12–13)

Geshurites (Joshua 13:13)

Maachathites (Joshua 13:13)

Amorites (Judges 1:35)

Jebusites (Judges 1:19–21)

Lord made a covenant with Abram, giving which lands to his descendants? Genesis 15:18–21

Kenites

Rephaim

Kenizzites

Amorites

Kadmonites

Canaanites

Hittites

Girgashites

Perizzites

Jebusites

Women of the Bible

What unnamed daughters' contributions made a difference in Bible history?

Lot's daughters (Gen. 19:12, 14)

Pharaoh's daughter who adopted Moses (Exod. 2:10)

Jephthah's daughter (Judges 11:34, 40)

Pharaoh's daughter, the wife of Solomon (1 Kings 7:8)

Daughters of Zion (Zech. 9:9)

Jairus' daughter (Matt. 9:18–25)

Herodias' daughter (Matt. 14:6)

Canaanite daughter (Matt. 15:22)

Daughters of Jerusalem weeping for Jesus (Luke 23:28)

Philip's four daughters (Acts 21:8–9)

What unnamed wives' contributions made a difference in Bible history?
Cain's wife (Gen. 4:17)
Potiphar's wife (Gen. 39:7–12)
Noah's wife and his sons' wives (Gen. 7:13)
Solomon's wife (1 Kings 9:16)
Naaman's wife (2 Kings 5:2–4)
Manoah's wife (Judges 13:2)
Job's wife (Job 2:9)
Moses' Ethiopian/Cushite wife (Num. 12:1)
Lot's wife (Luke 17:32)

What unnamed women made contributions that made a difference in Bible history?
Wise-hearted woman (Exod. 35:22–29)
Woman of Thebez (Judges 9:50–57)
Four hundred virgins of Jabesh-Gilead (Judges 21)
Mephibosheth's nurse (2 Sam. 4:4)
Woman of Tekoah (2 Sam. 14:1–20)
Widow woman (1 Kings 4:1–7)
Zarephath widow woman (1 Kings 17:7–16)
Woman of Shunem (2 Kings 4:8–37)
Samaritan woman (John 4:42)
Syrophoenician/Canaanite woman (Matt. 15:21–28)

What slave women were concubines of Bible patriarchs?
Reumah of Nahor (Gen. 22:23–24)
Zilpah of Jacob (Gen. 37:2)
Bilhah of Jacob (Gen. 37:2)
Hagar of Abraham (Gen. 25:12)
Rizpah of Saul (2 Sam. 3:7)
Keturah of Abraham (1 Chron. 1:32)
Ephah of Caleb (1 Chron. 2:46, 48)
Maachah of Caleb (1 Chron. 2:46, 48)
Timna of Eliphaz (Gen. 36:12)

Who were handmaids or considered herself as a handmaid?

Hagar (Sarai) (Gen. 16:1)

Zilpah (Leah) (Gen. 29:24)

Bilhah (Rachel) (Gen. 29:29)

Ruth (Boaz) (Ruth 3:9)

Hannah (Samuel) (1 Sam. 1:18)

Woman of Endor (Saul) (1 Sam. 28:21–24)

Wise woman (Joab) (2 Sam. 20:17)

Bathsheba (David) (1 Kings 1:13)

Shunammite woman (Elisha) (2 Kings 4:16)

Mary (Lord) (Luke 1:38)

What women of the Bible are associated with the number seven?

Rachel—Jacob worked seven years (Gen. 29:20)

Leah—Jacob worked seven years (Gen. 29:30)

Zipporah—one of seven sisters and Moses' wife (Exod 2:16)

Miriam—put out for seven days with leprosy (Num. 12:15)

Ruth—better than seven sons (Ruth 4:15)

Hannah—barren but bore seven children (1 Sam. 2:5)

Shunammite woman—son sneezed seven times (2 Kings 4:35)

Esther—seven handmaids (Esther 2:9)

Anna—husband died after seven years of marriage (Luke 2:36)

Mary Magdalene—delivered of seven demons (Luke 8:2)

What woman helped a man in the Bible?

Woman in Bahurin hid Jonathan and Ahimaaz in a well cover with corn (2 Sam. 17:17–21)

Rahab helped two spies hide in the rooftop (Joshua 2:4–5)

Jael killed Sisera with a tent nail for Barak (Judges 4:21–22)

Michal helped David escape from Saul (1 Sam. 19:12–14)

Widow of Zarephath sustained Elijah with food (1 Kings 17:9–16)

Woman of Shunem made a chamber and offered food to Elisha (2 Kings 4:8–11)

Israelite little maid advised Naaman to see a prophet in Samaria (2 Kings 5:1)

What women bowed down before men?
Ruth (Ruth 2:10)
Abigail (1 Sam. 25:23)
Bathsheba (1 Kings 1:16)
Shunammite Woman (2 Kings 4:37)

What is the mother's name of Judah's first ten kings?
Naamah—Rehoboam (1 Kings 14:31)
Maachah—Abijam (1 Kings 15:2)
Azubah—Jehoshaphat (1 Kings 22:42)
Athaliah—Ahaziah (2 Kings 8:26)
Jehoaddan—Amaziah (2 Kings 14:2)
Jecholiah—Azariah (2 Kings 15:2)
Jerusha—Jotham (2 Kings 15:33)
Hephzibah—Manasseh (2 Kings 21:1)
Meshullemeth—Amon (2 Kings 21:19)
Jedidah—Josiah (2 Kings 22:1)

What women wept or cried?
Hagar (Gen. 21:16)
Samson's wife (Judges 14:16)
Naomi (Ruth 1:9, 14)
Ruth (Ruth 1:9, 14)
Orpah (Ruth 1:9, 14)
Hannah (1 Sam. 1:7)
Mary (John 20:11)

Who conceived and bore a son?

Eve—Cain (Gen. 4:1)
Bilhah—Dan (Gen. 30:5)
Hagar—Ishmael (Gen. 16:4)
Tamar—Pharez (Gen. 38:18)
Sarah—Isaac (Gen. 21:2)
Jochebed—Moses (Exod. 2:2)
Rebekah—Esau (Gen. 25:21)

Ruth—Obed (Ruth 4:13–17)
Leah—Reuben (Gen. 29:32)
Hannah—Samuel (1 Sam. 1:20)
Shuah—Er (Gen. 38:3)
Gomer—Jezreel (Hosea 1:3, 4)
Mary—Jesus (Matt. 1:20)
Elizabeth—John (Luke 1:24)

What barren women experienced miraculous births?
Sarai (Sarah) (Gen. 11:30)
Rebekah (Gen. 25:21)
Rachel (Gen. 29:31)
Manoah's wife (Judges 13:2)
Hannah (1 Sam. 15:33)
Shunamite woman (2 Kings 4:8–17)
Elisabeth (Luke 1:7)

Who were virgins in the Bible?
Rebekah (Gen. 24:15)
Jephthah's daughter (Judges 11:37)
Tamar (2 Sam. 13:2)
Daughters of Zidon, Zion, Babylon (Isa. 23:12; 37:22)
Abishag (1 Kings 1:3)
Daughters of Egypt (Jer. 46:11)
Esther (Esther 2:17)
Daughters of Judah (Lam. 1:15)
Mary (Luke 1:27)
Philip's four daughters (Acts 21:8, 9)

Who were royal daughters?
Michal, daughter of King Saul (1 Sam. 18:27)
Maacah, daughter of King Talmai of Geshur (2 Sam. 3:3)
Jezebel, daughter of Ethbaal, King of the Zidonians (1 Kings 16:31)
Athaliah, daughter of Omri, King of Israel (2 Kings 8:26)
Jehosheba, daughter of King Joram (2 Kings 11:2)
Bithiah, daughter of Pharaoh (1 Chron. 4:18)

Who were daughters-in-law listed in the Bible?
Sarah—Terah (Gen. 11:31)
Tamar—Judah (Gen. 38:11)
Orpah—Naomi (Ruth 1:6–8)
Ruth—Naomi (Ruth 1:22)
Phinehas' wife—Eli (1 Sam. 4:19)

What woman were named Mary?

Mary mother of Jesus (Matt. 1:18)

Mary Magdalene (Luke 8:2)

Mary, sister of Martha (John 1:11)

Mary, wife of Cleophas (John 19:25)

Mary, mother of John Mark (Acts 12:12)

Bible Personalities with Connection to God

What men failed Jesus?

Herod felt threatened by Him (Matt. 2)

His own people who thought He was too commonplace (John 1)

Many of his disciples (Matt. 26:56)

Judas Iscariot (Matt. 27:3)

Peter denied him (Matt. 26:69–75)

False witnesses lied about Him (Matt. 26:59–62)

Pilate wanted to please the people (Matt. 27:11–26)

Soldiers who were calloused and hard hearted (Matt. 27:27–31)

Who provoked God to anger and made Israel to sin?

Jeroboam, son of Nebat (1 Kings 15:30)

Ahab (1 Kings 16:33)

Baasha, son of Nebat (1 Kings 21:22)

Manasseh (2 Kings 23:26)

Ephraim (Hosea 12:14)

Who built an altar unto the Lord?

Noah (Gen. 8:20)

Aaron (Exod. 32:5)

Abram (Gen. 12:7)/Abraham
(Gen. 22:9)

Bezaleel (Exod. 38:1)

Isaac (Gen. 26:25)

Balak (Num. 23:14)

Jacob (Gen. 35:7)

Joshua (Joshua 8:30)

Moses (Exod. 17:15)

Gideon (Judges 6:24)

Samuel (1 Sam. 7:17)

Ahab (1 Kings 16:30–32)

Saul (1 Sam. 14:35)

Elijah (1 Kings 18:32)

David (2 Sam. 24:25)

Urijah (2 Kings 16:11)

Solomon (1 Kings 7:48)

Jeshua and Zerubbabel
(Ezra 3:2)

Jeroboam (1 Kings 12:32, 33)

Children of Reuben
(Joshua 22:10)

Manasseh (Joshua 22:10)

Gad (Joshua 22:10)

King David (2 Sam.24:25)

King Saul (1 Sam. 14:35)

King Solomon (2 Chron. 8:12)

What men prophesied of the coming Messiah?

Micah (Micah 5:2)

Zechariah (Zech. 9:9)

Chief Priest and Scribes (Matt. 2:4–6)

John the Baptist (Mark 1:4–9)

Isaiah (Isa. 7:14)

David (Ps. 69:21)

What women are mentioned in Jesus Christ's lineage?

Tamar—Judah (Matt. 1:3)

Rahab—Salmon (Matt. 1:5)

Ruth—Boaz (Matt. 1:5)

Bathsheba—David (Matt. 1:6)

Mary—Joseph (Matt. 1:16)

What men are included in the genealogy of Jesus Christ before Solomon?
Matthew 1:2–6

Abraham	Boaz (Booz)
Aminadab	Perez (Phares)
Isaac	Obed
Hagshon (Naasson)	Hezron (Esrom)
Jacob	Jesse
Salmon	Aram
Judah	David

To whom did God say "GO?"
Noah (Gen. 8:16)
Balaam (Num. 23:16)
Abram (Gen. 11:31)
Joshua (Joshua 8:1)
Jacob (Gen. 32:9)
Gideon (Judges 7:3–7)
Aaron (Exod. 4:27)
Samuel (1 Sam. 16:1)
Moses (Exod. 9:1)
David (1 Chron. 14:10)
Isaac (Gen. 26:2)

Who in the Old Testament had an encounter with the angel of the Lord?

Hagar (Gen. 16:9)	Zechariah (Zech. 1:9)
Abraham (Gen. 22:11, 15)	Joshua (Zech. 3:6)
Jacob (Gen. 32:1)	Manoah's wife (Judges 13:3)
Moses (Exod. 3:2)	Gideon (Judges 6:22)
Balaam (Num 22:34–35)	Joseph (Matt. 1:24)
David (2 Sam. 24:16–17)	Philip (Acts 8:26)
Elijah (2 Kings 1:15)	Peter (Acts 12:7)

What Bible characters did the Lord God "call" for?

Adam (Gen. 3:9)

Moses (Exod. 3:4)

Aaron and Miriam (Num. 12:5)

Samuel (1 Sam. 3:4)

Israelites (Isa. 42:6)

What Bible characters called upon the Lord God?

Hagar (Gen. 16:13)

Abram/Abraham (Gen. 21:33)

Samson (Judges 15:18)

Samuel (1 Sam. 1:18)

David (1 Chron. 21:26)

Jabez (1 Chron. 4:10)

Jeremiah (Lam. 3:55)

Fill in the blank with a Bible character other than a king or prophet: "And the Lord said unto"

Cain (Gen. 4:6)

Noah (Gen. 7:1)

Abram (Gen. 13:14)/Abraham (Gen. 18:13)

Rebekah (Gen. 25:23)

Jacob (Gen. 31:3)

Moses (Exod. 4:4)

Aaron (Exod. 4:27)

Joshua (Joshua 3:7)

Gideon (Judges 7:7)

Satan (Job 1:7)

To whom did God say: "Fear Not?"
Abram (Gen. 15:1)
Isaac (Gen. 26:24)
Jacob (Gen. 46:3)
Joshua (Joshua 8:1)
Gideon (Judges 6:10)
Daniel (Dan. 10:19)
Judah/Israel (Zech. 8:13)
John (Rev. 1:17)

To whom did the Angel of God say: "Fear Not?"
Hagar (Gen. 21:17)
Mary, mother of Jesus (Luke 1:30)
Joseph (Matt. 1:20)
Shepherds (Luke 2:10)
Mary Magdalene (Matt. 28:5)
Paul (Acts 27:24)
Zachariah (Luke 1:13)

What patriarch who was faithful in God is listed in Hebrews 11?
Abel
Isaac
Enoch
Jacob
Noah
Joseph
Abraham
Moses
Sarah
Rahab

Who bowed down to worship the Lord?
> Abraham (Gen. 18:2)
> Lot (Gen. 19:1)
> Isaac's servant (Gen. 24:48)
> Moses (Exod. 34:8)
> Balaam (Num. 22:31)
> Joshua (Joshua 5:14)
> Samson (Judges 16:30)
> Jehoshaphat (2 Chron. 20:18)
> King Hezekiah (2 Chron. 29:30)
> Ezra (Neh. 8:6)

Who "did that which was right" in the sight of the Lord?
> David (1 Kings 11:38)
> Asa, son of Abijam (1 Kings 15:9)
> Jehoshaphat, son of Asa (1 Kings 22:43)
> Hezekiah, son of Ahaz (2 Kings 18:1–3)
> Joash, son of Jehoahaz (2 Kings 14:3)
> Amaziah, son of Joash (2 Kings 14:1–3)
> Josiah, son of Jedidah (2 Kings 22:1–2)
> Azariah (Uzziah), son of Amaziah (2 Kings 15:1–3)
> Jotham, son of Uzziah (2 Kings 15:32–34)

To whose prayers in the Old Testament did God answer "YES?"
> Abraham (Gen. 20:17)
> Moses (Num. 11:2)
> Hannah (1 Sam. 1:27)
> Nehemiah (Neh. 1:4; 2:8)
> Elisha (2 Kings 6:17–18)
> Hezekiah (2 Kings 20:1–6)
> Solomon (2 Chron. 7:1, 12)
> Manasseh (2 Chron. 33:13)
> David (Ps. 66:19)

To whose prayers in the New Testament did God answer "YES?"

John (Acts 8:14–17)

Peter (Acts 9:40)

Cornelius (Acts 10:20)

Paul (Acts 28:8)

Who fell down to worship God?

Balaam (Num. 22:31)

Moses (Deut. 9:25)

Job (Job 1:20)

Ezekiel (Ezek. 11:13)

Peter (Luke 5:8)

Jairus (Luke 8:41)

Mary, brother of Lazarus (John 11:32)

Ananias (Acts 5:5)

Stephen (Acts 7:59, 20)

Elijah (Elias) (James 5:17–18)

John the Revelator (Rev. 22:8)

What babies in the Bible were a gift promised by God?

Samson—Manoah's wife (Judges 13:3)

Jacob and Isau—Rebecca/Isaac (Gen. 25:21)

Isaac—Sarah/Abraham (Gen. 17:17)

Joseph and Benjamin—Rachel/Jacob (Gen. 30:22)

Shunammite son—Shunammite (2 Kings 4:15–17)

Samuel—Hannah (1 Sam. 1:17–20)

Jesus—Mary/Joseph (Matt. 1:20)

What harp players were in the house of the Lord?

Jubal (Gen. 4:21)

David (2 Sam. 16:23)

Asaph (1 Chron. 25:1)

Heman (1 Chron. 25:1)

Jeduthun (1 Chron. 25:1)

In Romans 16, who did Paul introduce to Phoebe and greet fellow workers in Christ Jesus?

Priscilla	Persis
Junia	Nereus
Aquila	Olympus
Amplias	Rufus
Epaenetus	Asyncirtus
Urbanus	Timotheus
Mary	Lucius
Stachys	Phlegon
Andronicus	Patrobas
Apelles	Jason
Tryphena	Sosipater
Tryphosa	Hermas
Philologus	Hermes
Julia	Gaius
Herodion	Eratus

Who were the Friends of the Lord God?

Moses (Exod. 33:11)
Lazarus (John 11:11)
Job (Job 29:4)
Publicans and sinners (Matt. 11:19)
Abraham (Isa. 41:8)
Anyone who does His commandments (John 15:14)
Judas (Matt. 26:47, 50)

Who "walked with God?"

Enoch (Gen. 5:22)
Noah (Gen. 6:9)
Meshach (Dan. 3:23–25)
Abednego (Dan. 3:23–25)
Shadrach (Dan. 3:23–25)
Levi (Mal. 2:4–6)

Who was called by God and replied, "Here I am?"
Abraham (Gen. 22:1, 11)
Samuel (1 Sam. 3:4–6)
Jacob (Gen. 46:2)
Isaiah (Isa. 6:8)
Moses (Exod. 3:4)
Ananias (Acts 9:10)

What people knelt and bowed down to worship Jesus?
Leader of the synagogue (Matt 9:18)
Syrophoenician woman (Mark 7:25)
Mary Magdalene and others (Matt 28.9)
Simon Peter (Luke 5:8)
Eleven disciples (Matt 28:17)
One of ten lepers (Luke 17:16)
The unclean spirit (Mark 3:11)
Mary (John 11:32)
Woman who had an issue of blood (Mark 5:33)

Who preached and called for repentance, saying: "turn to me/God?"
Nehemiah (Neh. 1:9)
Haggai (Hag 2:17)
Joel (Joel 2:12)
Zechariah (Zech. 1:3)
Isaiah (Isa. 44:22)
Malachi (Mal. 3:7)
Jeremiah (Jer. 4:1)
Paul (Acts 26:20)

God came to or revealed Himself to whom by dream or vision by night?

Abimelech (Gen. 20:3)

Jacob (Gen. 46:2)

Laban the Syrian (Gen. 31:24)

Butler and Cupbearer (Gen. 40:5)

The Baker (Gen. 40:5)

Solomon (1 Kings 3:5)

Daniel (Dan. 2:19)

Paul (Acts 18:9)

To whom did God appear by night?

Isaac (Gen. 26:24)

Gideon (Judges 6:25)

Moses (Exod. 12:31)

Aaron (Exod. 12:31)

Solomon (2 Chron. 1:7)

Balaam (Num. 22:20)

Nathan (2 Sam. 7:14)

To whom did an Angel of the Lord speak?

Abraham (Gen. 22:11)

Jacob (Gen. 31:11)

Balaam (Num. 22:35)

Gideon (Judges 6:12)

Manoah (Joshua 13:13)

Elijah (2 King 1:15)

Zechariah (Zech. 1:9)

Zacharias (Luke 1:13)

Peter (Acts 12:8)

John (Rev. 17:7)

To whom did God say: "I will be with you (thee)?"

Isaac (Gen. 26:3)

Jacob (Gen. 31:3)

Moses (Exod. 3:12)

Joshua (Joshua 1:5; Joshua 3:7)

David (1 Kings 11:38)

Gideon (Judges 6:16)

To whom did the Angel of the Lord appear?

Moses (Exod. 3:2)

Gideon (Judges 6:12)

Manoah's wife (Judges 13:3)

Shepherds (Luke 2:15)

Joseph (Jesus' father) (Matt. 1:20)

Zacharias (Luke 1:11)

Who received/heard a voice from heaven?

Hagar (Gen. 21:17)

Nebuchadnezzar (Dan. 4:31)

The alive generation (1 Thes. 4:16)

Jesus (Matt. 3:17)

Peter (Acts 11:7–9)

John the revelator, Rev. 14:13

To whom did Jesus say, "Follow Me?"

Peter (Matt. 4:18–19)

Disciples (Matt. 16:24)

Andrew (Matt. 4:18–19)

Rich young ruler (Matt. 19:16–22)

Scribe (Matt. 8:18–22)

Multitude following Jesus (Luke 14:27)

Matthew (Matt. 9:9)

Philip (John 1:43)

Who said "Lord, have mercy?"

David (Ps. 6:2; 9:13)

Isaiah (Isa. 49:13)

Angel of the Lord (Zech. 1:12)

Two blind men (Matt. 20:30)

Canaanite women (Matt. 15:22)

Father of possessed son (Matt. 17:15)

Who, other than prophetic Bible authors, claimed that the "Word of the Lord" came to them?

Abram (Gen. 15:1)

Moses (Exod. 4:28)

Nathan (2 Sam. 7:4)

Gad, the Prophet (2 Sam. 24:11)

Solomon (1 Kings 6:11)

Jehu (1 Kings 16:1)

Elijah (1 Kings 21:17)

David (1 Chron. 22:8)

Shemaiah (2 Chron. 11:2)

"The word of the Lord" is against what?

Altar in Bethel (1 Kings 13:32)

Saul (1 Chron. 10:13)

Baasha (1 Kings 16:7)

Gentiles (Jer. 46:1)

Chaldees and Syrians (2 Kings 24:2)

Philistines (Jer. 47:1)

Moabites (2 Kings 24:2)

Elam (Jer. 49:34)

Children of Ammon and Judah (2 Kings 24:2)

Cherethites nation by the sea coast (Zeph. 2:5)

Who asked if Jesus was the Son of God?

Satan (Matt. 4:3)

Caiaphas, high priest (Matt. 26:63)

Chief priests, with the scribes and elders and crowd (Matt. 27:43)

Nathanael (John 1:49)

Nebuchadnezzar (Dan. 3:25)

Who recognized that Jesus was the Son of God?

Unclean spirit (Matt. 8:28–29)

John (John 1:34)

Jesus' disciples and Peter (Matt. 14:33)

Martha (John 11:27)

Mark (Mark 1:1)

Luke (Luke 3:3)

Cornelius and soldier (Matt. 27:54)

Jews (John 19:7)

Angel Gabriel (Luke 1:35)

Philip (Acts 8:37)

Devil (Luke 4:41)

Paul/Saul (Acts 9:20)

Who said to hear the "Word of the Lord?"

Joshua (Joshua 3:9)

Jeremiah (Jer. 44:24)

Samuel (1 Sam. 15:1)

Ezekiel (Ezek. 13:2)

Michaiah (1 Kings 22:19)

Hosea (Hosea 4:1)

Elisha (2 Kings 7:1)

Amos (Amos 7:16)

Isaiah (Isa. 39:5)

Who referred to Jesus as the "Son of David?"
    Matthew (Matt. 1:1)
    Pharisees (Matt. 22:42)
    Two blind men (Matt. 9:27)
    Blind Bartimaeus (Mark 10:47)
    Woman of Canaan (Matt. 15:22)
    Scribes (Mark 12:35)
    Multitudes of people [to Jerusalem] (Matt. 21:9, 15)

Who told the "Word of the Lord" to a large group of people?
    Moses to Israel (Exod. 24:3)
    Joshua to Israel (Joshua 24:27)
    Samuel to Israel (1 Sam. 8:10)
    Jeremiah to the people of Judah (Jer. 44:24)
    Isaiah to the people of Jerusalem (Isa. 28:14)

Who hearkened to the "Voice of the Lord?"
    Adam and Eve (Gen. 3:8)
    Johanan (Jer. 43:4)
    Moses (Exod. 15:26)
    Zerubbabel, son of Shealtiel (Hag, 1:12)
    Isaiah (Isa. 6:8)
    Joshua, son of Josedech (Hag. 1:12)
    Jeremiah (Jer. 38:20)
    Moses (Acts 7:31)

Who ignored/rejected "the Word of the Lord?"
    Balaam (Num. 22:18)
    People of Judah (Jer. 6:10)
    Pharaoh (Exod. 9:21)
    Religious leaders (Jer. 8:9)
    Saul (1 Sam. 15:23, 26)
    Zedekiah (Jer. 37:2)
    Unnamed prophet (1 Kings 20:35)

Who told the "Word of the Lord" to another person?

Balaam unto Balak (Num. 22:18)

Jeremiah unto Cyrus, King of Persia (Ezra 1:1)

Samuel unto Saul (1 Sam. 15:1)

Jeremiah unto Zedekiah (Jer. 34:4)

Micaiah to King Jehoshaphat's messenger (1 Kings 22:13)

Jeremiah unto Baruch (Jer. 36:4)

Isaiah unto Hezekiah (Isa. 39:5)

Haggai unto Zerubbabel (Hag. 1:1)

Hezekiah unto Isaiah (Isa. 39:8)

Haggai unto Joshua (Hag. 1:1)

To whom did God say, "be fruitful and multiply?"

Water creatures and winged fowl (Gen. 1:21, 22)

Adam and Eve (Gen. 1:27, 28)

Animals from Noah's Ark (Gen. 8:15–17)

Noah's family (Gen. 9:1)

Jacob (Gen. 35:9–11)

Who took away the treasures from the house of the Lord?

Shishak, king of Egypt (1 Kings 14:25–26)

Ahaz king of Judah (2 Kings 16:8)

King Asa (1 Kings 15:18)

Hezekiah gave to Assyrian King (2 Kings 18:15)

Jehoash, king of Judah (2 Kings 12:18)

Nebuchadnezzar, king of Babylon (2 Kings 24:12–14)

Jehoash (Joash), king of Israel (2 Kings 14:13–14)

Who was mentioned as being filled with the Holy Spirit/Ghost?

John the Baptist (Luke 1:13–15)

Saul/Paul (Acts 13:9)

Elisabeth (Luke 1:41)

Barnabas (Acts 11:24)

Zacharias (Luke 1:67)

The Lord's follower at Penticost (Acts 2:4)

Peter (Acts 4:8)

Peter and John with group of believers (Acts 4:31)

Stephen (Act 6:5)

Jesus' Disciples (Acts 13:52)

Who was killed by the Lord in an extraordinary way?

Lot's wife—pillar of salt (Gen. 19:26)

Korah and company—swallowed by the earth (Num. 16:32)

Nadab—fire from heaven (Lev. 10:2)

Abihu—fire from heaven (Lev. 10:2)

Jehoram—incurable disease (2 Chron. 21:18–19)

Azariah—smote with leprosy (2 Kings 15:5)

Ashdod—smote with emerods (1 Sam. 5:6)

Herod—eaten by worms (Acts 12:21–23)

Who was killed by the Lord in an unspecified manner?

Er (Gen. 38:7–10)

First child of David and Bath-sheba (2 Sam. 12:15)

Onan (Gen. 38:7–10)

Saul (1 Chron. 10:13–14)

Nabal (1 Sam. 25:38)

Jeroboam (1 Chron. 13:15, 20)

Uzzah (2 Sam. 6:7)

What person in the Bible was called a "man of God?"

Moses (Deut. 33:1)

Elisha (2 Kings 4:1, 7)

Samuel (1 Sam. 9:6, 14)

David (2 Chron. 8:14)

Shemaiah (1 Kings 12:22)

Hanan (Jer. 35:5)

Elijah (1 Kings 17:18)

What Old Testament men had their name come from God?

Adam (Gen. 1:19)

Ishmael (Gen. 16:11)

Isaac (Gen. 17:19)

Israel (Gen. 32:28)

Josiah (1 Kings 13:2)

Solomon (1 Chron. 22:9)

Mahershalalhashbaz (Isa. 8:3)

Jezreel (Hosea 1:2–4)

Loammi (Hosea 1:8–9)

To what Old Testament man who was not a prophet did God speak?

Adam (Gen. 2:16)

Cain (Gen. 4:6)

Noah (Gen. 6:13)

Abram/Abraham (Gen. 13:14)

Jacob (Gen. 35:1)

Moses (Exod. 3:14)

Aaron (Exod. 4:27)

Joshua (Joshua 3:7)

Gideon (Judges 7:2)

David (1 Chron. 28:2–3)

Who read God's word?
> Josiah (2 Kings 23:2)
> Shaphan (2 Kings 22:8)
> Ezra (Neh. 8:2, 3)
> Levites (Neh. 8:7–9)
> Children of Israel (Neh. 9:1–3)
> Seraiah (Jer. 51:51–63)
> Jesus (Luke 4:14–20)
> Ethiopian eunuch (Acts 8:27–33)
> Moses (2 Cor. 3:5)

Who was sealed by the Living God? Revelation 7:2–8

Judah	Asher
Manasses	Issachar
Reuben	Nephthalim
Simeon	Zabulon
Gad	Joseph
Levi	Benjamin

Who did the Lord call "my servant?"
> Abraham (Gen. 26:24)
> Moses (Num. 12:7–8)
> Caleb (Num. 14:24)
> David (2 Sam. 3:18)
> Job (Job 1:8)
> Isaiah (Isa. 20:3)
> Eliakim (Isa. 20:20)
> Jacob (Israel) (Isa. 41:8–9)
> Nebuchadnezzar (Jer. 25:9)
> Zerubbabel (Hag. 2:23)

Who were known as servants of the Lord Jesus?
Isaac (Exod. 32:13)
Joshua (Exod. 33:11)
Ahijah (1 Kings 14:18)
Elijah (1 Kings 18:36)
Jonah (2 Kings 14:25)
Paul (Titus 1:1)
James (James 1:1)
Simon Peter (2 Peter 1:1)
Jude (Jude 1:1)
John (Rev. 1:1)

The Spirit of the Lord came upon whom?
Othniel (Judges 3:1)
Gideon (Judges 6:34)
Jephthah (Judges 11:29)
Samson (Judges 14:6)
David (1 Sam. 16:13)

Fill in the blanks with a Bible character and an action: "_____" was told to "_____" the Lord "with all your heart."
Moses—love (Deut. 11:13)
Joshua—serve (Joshua 22:5)
Samuel—serve (1 Sam. 12:20)
Jeremiah—search (Jer. 29:13)
Joel—turn to me (Joel 2:12)

Who was stricken by God?

Men outside Lot's house with blindness (Gen. 19:11)

Nadab and Abihu were killed (Lev. 10:1–3)

Jereboam's hand withered (1 Kings 13:4)

Gehazi became a leper (2 Kings 5:27)

Miriam with leprosy (Num. 12:10)

Uzziah with leprosy (2 Chron. 26:18–21)

Egyptians died (1 Sam. 4:8)

Uzzah died—touched the ark (2 Sam. 6:7)

Herod eaten by worms died (Acts 12:23)

What people tried to destroy or kill Jesus?

Pharisees (Matt. 12:14)

Herodians (Mark 3:6)

Jews/Jewish council (Matt. 2:4)

Scribes (Mark 11:8)

Chief priest (Matt. 25:20)

Chief priest, scribes, and leaders (Luke 19:47)

To whom did Jesus say, "verily, verily, I say unto you...?"

Nathanael (John 1:49–51)

12 disciples (John 13:16)

Nicodemus (John 3:2–4)

Judas and disciples (John 13:21)

Jewish leaders (John 5:19)

Peter (John 13:38)

People (John 6:25–26)

Philip (John 14:12)

Andrew and Greeks (John 12:22–23)

Who made a "vow unto the Lord?"

Jacob (Gen. 28:20–22)

Absalom (2 Sam. 15:7–8)

Israel (Num. 21:2)

David (Ps. 61:8)

Jephthah (Judges 11:30–31)

Egyptians (Isa. 19:21)

Hannah (1 Sam. 1:11)

Elkanah (1 Sam. 1:21)

Sailors (Jonah 1:16)

What people chose to follow God even to death?

Esther (Esther 4)

Jeremiah (Jer. 26)

Daniel (Dan. 6)

Stephen (Acts 6:8–8:1)

Shadrach (Dan. 3)

Paul (2 Cor. 6:11–7:1)

Meshach (Dan. 3)

Peter (1 Peter 2:9)

Abednigo (Dan. 3)

Silas (Acts 16)

Barnabas (Acts 16)

John (Acts 16)

Places

What are the names of cities mentioned in Genesis?
    Arbah (Gen. 35:27)
    Luz (Gen. 28::19)
    Avith (Gen. 36:35)
    Pau (Gen. 36:39)
    Beersheba (Gen. 26:33)
    Rehoboth (Gen. 10:11)
    Dinhabah (Gen. 36:32)
    Sodom (Gen. 19:4)
    Zoar (Gen. 19:22)

What are the names of the cities of refuge? Numbers 3
    Kadesh, in Naphtali
    Golan, in Bashan
    Shechem, on Mount Ephraim
    Ramoth-Gilead, in Gad
    Hebron, in Judah
    Bezer, in Reuben

What cities were burnt with fire?

Ai (Joshua 8:19)

Egypt (Ezek. 30:8)

Gaza (Amos 1:7)

Gezer (1 Kings 9:16)

Gibeah (Judges 20:48)

Gomorrah (Gen. 19:24)

Hazael (Amos 1:4)

Jerusalem (Judges 1:8)

Judah (Amos 2:5)

Laish or Dan (Judges 18:27)

Magog (Ezek. 39:6)

Midian (Num. 31:10)

Moab (Amos 2:2)

Rabbah (Amos 1:14)

Shechem (Judges 9:49)

Sihon (Num. 21:28)

Sodom (Gen. 19:24)

Teman (Amos 1:12)

Tyrus (Amos 1:10)

Zoam (Ezek. 30:14)

What names of cities mentioned in the New Testament?

Arimathaea (Luke 23:51)

Babylon (Rev. 18:10)

Bethlehem (Luke 2:4)

Bethsaida (John 1:44)

Capernaum (Luke 4: 31)

Jerusalem (Luke 24:49)

Joppa (Acts 11:5)

Thyatira (Acts 16:14)

Lasea (Acts 27:8)

Myra (Acts 27:5)

Nain (Luke 7:11)

Sidon (Luke 4:26)

Sychar (John 4:5)

Tarsus (Acts 21:39)

What Philistine cities representing their rulers sent gold tumors as guilt offerings? 1 Samuel 6:4, 17

Ashdod

Gaza

Ashkelon

Gath

Ekron

At what places did the Israelites stop and camp after leaving Egypt?
Numbers 33:6–48

Succoth	Benejaakan	Punon
Makheloth	Dophkah	Rimmonparez
Etham	Horhagidgad	Oboth
Tahath	Alush	Libna
Migdol at Pihahiroth	Jotbathah	Ijeabarim/Ilim
	Rephidim	Rissah
Tarah	Eziongaber	Dibongad
Marah	Desert of Sinai	Kehelathah
Mithcah	Kadesh	Almondiblathaim
Elim	Kibrothhattaavah	Mount Shapher
Hashmonah	Mount Hor	Mount Abarim
Red Sea	Hazeroth	Haradah
Moseroth	Zalmonah	Moab near Jericho
Wilderness of Sin	Rithmah	

To what major places did Jesus travel?

Bethany (John 12:1)
Galilee (Matt. 4:12)
Bethlehem (Matt. 2:1)
Jericho/Jordan (Mark 10:46)
Cana (John 2:1)
Jerusalem (Luke 2:22)
Capernaum (Matt. 4:13)
Nazareth (Luke 2:39–40)
Egypt (Matt. 2:14)
Samaria/Judea (John 4:3, 4)
Bethsaida (Luke 9:10)
Mount Olives

Caesarea Philippi (Matt. 16:13)
Nain (Luke 7:11)
Gadarenes (Decapolis) (Matt. 8:28)
Sidon (Matt. 15:21)
Gennesaret (Matt. 14:34)
Sychar (John 4:5)
Gethsemane (Matt. 26:36)
Temples/Synagogues
Golgotha (Matt. 27:33)
Tyre (Matt. 15:21)
Magdala/Magadan (Matt. 15:39)

To what mountains did the Israelites travel?
Sephar (Gen. 10:30)
Seir (Gen. 14:6)
Gilead (Gen. 31:21)
Sinai (Exod. 19:11)
Horeb (Exod. 33:6)
Hor (Num. 20:22)
Shapher (Num. 33:23)
Sion (Deut. 4:48)
Nebo (Deut. 32:49)
Paran (Deut. 33:2)

To what mountains did David go?
Tabor (Judges 4:12)
Carmel (1 Kings 18:20)
Zalmon (Judges 9:48)
Zion (2 Kings 19:31)
Gilboa (1 Sam. 31:1)
Moriah (2 Chron. 3:1)
Olivet (2 Sam. 15:30)

What mountains did Joshua and the Israelites conquer?
Ebal (Deut. 11:29)
Gerizim (Deut. 27:12)
Halak (Joshua 12:5)
Hermon (Joshua 12:5)
Ephron (Joshua 15:9)
Jearim (Joshua 15:10)
Baalah (Joshua 15:11)
Bethel (Joshua 16:1)
Ephraim (Joshua 17:15)
Heres (Judges 1:35)

What places in the Old Testament Bible still have the same name today?

Egypt (Gen. 12:10)

Jordan (Gen. 13:10)

Damascus (Gen. 14:15)

Israel (Gen. 32:28)

Lebanon (Deut. 1:7)

Syria (Judges 10:6)

India (Esther 1:1)

Ethiopia (Esther 1:1)

Palestine (Joel 3:4)

Libya (Ezek. 30:5)

Greece (Zech. 9:13)

What places in the New Testament Bible still have the same name today?

Rome (Acts 2:10)

Athens (Acts 17:15)

Cyprus (Acts 4:36)

Italy (Acts 18:2)

Macedonia (Acts 16:9)

Alexandria (Acts 18:24)

What is the name of a place that remains "unto this day," according to the Bible?

Beersheba (Gen. 26:33)

Mahanehdan (Judges 18:12)

Gilgal (Joshua 5:9)

Absalom's place (2 Sam. 18:18)

The valley of Anchor (Joshua 7:26)

Land of Cabul (1 Kings 9:13)

Luz (Judges 1:26)

Valley of Berachah (2 Chron. 20:26)

Havothjair (Judges 10:4)

Jehovahshalom (Judges 6:24)

What city's destruction was foretold?

Sodom (Gen. 19:1)

Gomorrah (Gen. 19:24)

Tyrus (Ezek. 26:4–5)

Nineveh (Jonah 1:1–2)

Jerusalem (Luke 21:20)

Babylon (Rev. 18:21)

What places in the Bible had a famine?

Haran (Gen. 12:10)

Over all the face of the earth (Gen. 41:56)

Bethlehem (Ruth 1:1)

Samaria (1 Kings 18:2)

Gilgal (2 Kings 4:38)

Egypt and Canaan (Acts 7:11)

Jerusalem (Jer. 52:1–6)

What are names of hills found in the Bible?

Gaash (Joshua 24:30)

Moreh (Judges 7:1)

Hachilah (1 Sam. 23:19)

Ammah (2 Sam. 2:24)

Samaria (1 Kings 16:26)

Zion (Ps. 2:6)

Mizar (Ps. 42:6)

Bashan (Ps. 68:15)

Jerusalem (Isa. 10:32)

Goath (Jer. 31:39)

What are names of wildernesses in the Bible

Beersheba (Gen. 21:14)

Bethaven (Joshua 18:12)

Damascus (1 Kings 19:15)

Edom (2 Kings 3:18)

Egypt (Ezek. 20:36)

Engedi (1 Sam. 24:1)

Etham (Num. 33:8)

Gibeon (2 Sam. 2:24)

Jeruel (2 Chron. 20:16)

Judea (Judges 1:16)

Judah (Matt. 3:1)

Kadesh (Ps. 29:8)

Kedemoth (Deut. 2:26)

Moab (Duet. 2:8)

Paran (Gen. 21:21)

Red Sea (Exod. 13:18)

Shur (Exod. 15:22)

Sin (Exod. 16:1)

Sinai (Exod. 19:1)

Tekoa (2 Chron. 20:20)

Zin (1 Sam. 23:14)

Ziph (Num. 13:21)

What towers are named in the Bible?

Tower of Edar (Gen. 35:21)

Tower of Penuel (Judges 8:17)

Tower of Shechem (Judges 9:46–49)

Tower in Jezreel (2 Kings 9:17)

Tower of Meah (Neh. 3:1)

Tower of Hananeel (Neh. 3:1)

Tower of David (Song of Sol. 7:4

Tower of Syene (Ezek. 29:10)

Tower of Siloam (Luke 13:4)

In what places was a trumpet heard blown?

Mountain of Ephraim (Judges 3:27)

Tekoa (Jeremiah 6:1)

Solemn feast day (Ps. 81:3)

Ramah (Hosea 5:8)

In the land (Jer. 4:5)

Zion (Joel 2:1)

Jericho (Joshua 6:20)

To what people or groups was Israel in bondage and forced to serve?

Pharaoh, King of Egypt (Exod. 1:13)

Chushanrishathaim, King of Mesopotamia (Judges 3:8)

Eglon, King of Moab (Judges 3:14)

Jabin, King of Canaan (Judge 4:2, 3)

Midianites (Judges 6:1)

Ammonites (Judges 10:6–8)

Philistines (Judges 13:1)

Hazael, King of Syria (2 Kings 13:3)

Of what valleys did Joshua take control?

Achor (Joshua 7:24)

Jiphthahel (Joshua 19:14)

Ajalon (Joshua 10:12)

Keziz (Joshua 18:21)

Gibeon (Isa. 28:21)

Lebanon (Joshua 11:17)

Hinnom (Joshua 18:16)

Mizpeh (Joshua 11:8)

Jezreel (Joshua 17:16)

Fill in the blank with a word that is not a location: "Valley of ____."

Mountains (Zech. 14:5)

Craftsmen (Neh. 11:35)

Passengers (Ezek. 39:11)

Dead bodies (Jer. 31:40)

The shadow of death (Ps. 23:4)

Decision (Joel 3:14)

Slaughter (Jer. 7:32)

Giants on the north
 (Joshua 18:16)

Vision (Isa. 22:5, 12)

Baca (Ps. 84:6)

Berachah (2 Chron. 20:26)

Elah (1 Sam. 17:2)

Eshcol (Num. 32:9)

Gerar (Gen. 26:17)

Hamongog (Ezek. 39:15)

Jericho (Deut. 34:3)

Megiddo (2 Chron. 35:22)

Megiddon (Zech. 12:11)

Rephaim (2 Sam. 5:18)

Salt (2 Sam. 8:13)

Shaveh (Gen. 14:17)

Shittim (Joel 3:18)

Sorek (Judges 16:14)

Succoth (Ps. 60:6)

Zared (Num. 21:12)

Zephathah (2 Chron. 14:10)

Fill in the blank: The "Daughters of (*place*)____" are called virgins?

Zion (2 Kings 19:21)

Israel (Jer. 18:13)

Zidon (Isa. 23:12)

Egypt (Jer. 36:11)

Babylon (Isa. 47:1)

Judah (Lam. 1:15)

What are the names of islands mentioned in the Bible?

Tarshish (Isa. 23:6)

Chittim (Jer. 2:10)

Elishah (Ezek. 27:6–7)

Paphos (Acts 13:6)

Clauda (Acts 27:16)

Melita (Malta) (Acts 28:1)

Patmos (Rev. 1:9)

What were the rivers in the Garden of Eden? Genesis 2:10–14

Pison

Gihon

Hiddekel

Euphrates

What were the names of brooks or streams in the Bible?

Eshcol (Num. 13:23–24)

Arnon (Num. 21:14)

Zered (Deut. 2:13–14)

Besor (1 Sam. 20:9–10)

Kidron (2 Sam. 23:30)

Gaash (2 Sam. 23:30)

Cherith (1 Kings 17:3)

Kishon (1 Kings 18:40)

Kison (Ps. 83:9)

Cedron (John 18:1)

What are names of rivers in the Bible?

Pison (Gen. 2:11)
Gihon (Gen. 2:13)
Hiddekel (Gen. 2:14)
Euphrates (Gen. 2:14)
River of Egypt (Gen. 15:18)
Jordan (Gen. 32:10)
Arnon (Deut. 2:24)
Jabbok (Deut. 2:37)

Kanan (Joshua 16:8)
Kishon (Judges 4:7)
Abana (2 Kings 5:12)
Pharpar (2 Kings 5:12)
Gozan (2 Kings 17:6)
Ahava (Ezra 8:21)
Chebar (Ezek. 1:1)
Ulai (Dan. 8:2)

What pools were named in the Bible?

Pool of Gibeon (2 Sam. 2:13)
Pool of Samaria (1 Kings 22:38)
Pool of Siloah (Neh. 3:15)
Pool of Siloam (John 9:7)
Pool of Bethesda (John 5:2)

What bodies of water are listed in the Bible?

Waters of Egypt (Exod. 8:6)
Water of the well of
  Bethlehem (2 Sam. 23:15)
Waters of Marah
  (Exod. 15:23)
Waters of Israel (2 Kings 5:12)
Waters of Meribah
  (Deut. 33:8)
Waters of Shiloah (Isa. 8:6)
Waters of Merom
  (Joshua 11:5)
Waters of Nimrim (Isa. 15:6)
Waters of Jordan
  (Joshua 3:13)

Waters of Dimon (Isa. 15:9)
Waters of Enshemesh
  (Joshua 15:7)
Waters of Judah (Isa. 48:1)
Water of Jericho
  (Joshua 16:1)
Waters of Noah (Isa. 54:9)
Waters of Nephtoah
  (Joshua 18:15)
Waters of Sihor (Jer. 2:18)
Waters of Megiddo
  (Judges 5:19)
Waters of Kadesh
  (Ezek. 47:19)

What kinds of water are found in the Bible that are not the name of a place?

Waters of the flood (Gen. 7:7)

Waters of his cistern (2 Kings 18:31)

Water of thy pitcher/full cup (Gen. 24:17; Ps. 73:10)

Waters of the fountains (2 Chron. 32:3)

Water of the wells (Num. 20:17)

Waters of the lower old pool (Isa. 22:9, 11)

Water of the sea/Red sea (Exod. 15:19; Deut. 11:4)

Waters of the great deep (Isa. 51:10)

Water of the rain of heaven (Deut. 11:11)

Waters of the river (Dan. 12:6)

What is mentioned symbolically as the "Water of" something?

Water of purifying (Num. 8:7)

Water of strife (Ps. 106:32)

Water of separation (Num. 19:9)

Water of gall (Jer. 8:14)

Water of affliction (1 Kings 22:27)

Water of life (Rev. 22:1)

What places did Apostle Paul go on his first missionary journey? Acts 13–14

Depart from Antioch of Syria for Selucia

Salamis

Paphos

Perga in Pamphylia

Antioch in Pisidia

Iconium

Lystra city of Lycaonia

Derbe city of Lycaonia

Attalia

Returned to Antioch (of Syria)

What Canaanite inhabitants did the Israelites not force to leave their cities and they had to live among them?

Bethsean (Judges 1:27–35)

Zidon (Judges 1:31)

Taanach (Judges 1:27)

Ahlab (Judges 1:31)

Dor (Judges 1:27)

Achzib (Judges 1:31)

Ibleam (Judges 1:27)

Aphik (Judges 1:31)

Megiddo (Judges 1:27)

Helbah (Judges 1:31)

Gezer (Judges 1:29)

Rebob (Judges 1:31)

Kitron (Judges 1:30)

Beth-shemesh (Judges 1:33)

Nahalol (Judges 1:30)

Beth-anath (Judges 1:33)

Accho (Judges 1:31)

What were the name of the seven churches of Asia mentioned in Revelation?

Ephesus (Rev. 2:1)

Smyrna (Rev. 2:8)

Pergamos (Rev. 2:12)

Thyatira (Rev. 2:18)

Sardis (Rev. 3:1)

Philadelphia (Rev. 3:7)

Laodicea (Rev. 3:14)

Who built an altar and what was the place called?

EleloheIsrael, called/named by Jacob (Gen. 33:20)

Elbethel, called/named by Jacob (Gen. 35:7)

Jehovahnissi, called/named by Moses (Exod. 17:15)

Ed, called/named by Children of Reuben and Gad (Joshua 22:34)

Jehovahshalom, called/named by Gideon (Judges 6:24)

Things

What are the precious stones found in the New Jerusalem's foundation?
Revelation 21:19–20

Jasper

Sardius

Sapphire

Chrysolyte

Chalcedony

Beryl

Emerald

Topaz

Chrysoprasus

Jacinth

Sardonyx

Amethyst

What precious stones were found in the priest's breastplate?
Exodus 28:17–20

1st Row	*3rd Row*
Sardius	Ligure/Jacinth
Topaz	Agate
Carbuncle	Amethyst
2nd Row	*4th Row*
Emerald/Turquoise	Beryl
Sapphire	Onyx
Diamond	Jasper

What are names of metals mentioned in the Bible? Numbers 31:22; Ezra 8:27

Gold
Tin
Silver
Lead
Brass
Copper
Iron

What things made of iron could be found around a house, a temple, or a city in the Bible?

Bedstead (Deut. 3:11)
Furnace (Deut. 4:20)
Shoes (Deut. 33:25)
Fence (2 Sam. 23:7)
Pillars (Jer. 1:18)
Teeth (Dan. 7:7)
Pan (Ezek. 4:3)
Wall (Ezek. 4:3)
Gate (Acts 12:10)

What instruments of work or war were made of iron?

Yoke (Deut. 28:48)

Horns (1 Kings 22:11)

Chariots (Joshua 17:16)

Chains and fetters (Ps. 149:8)

Spear's head and other weapons (1 Sam. 17:7)

Pen (Jer. 17:1)

Harrows (pick) (2 Sam. 12:31)

Threshing instrument (Amos 1:3)

Nails (1 Chron. 22:3)

Rod (Rev. 2:27)

Axes (2 Sam. 12:31)

What things items in the Bible were made of silver?

Cup (Gen. 44:2)

Jewels (Exod. 3:22)

Gods/Idols (Exod. 20:23)

Bason (1 Chron. 28:17)

Sockets/Rings (Exod. 26:19)

Hooks (Exod. 27:10)

Chargers (Num. 7:13)

Trumpets (Num. 10:2)

Candlestick (1 Chron. 28:15)

Tables (1 Chron. 28:16)

Bowls (2 Kings 12:13)

Fillets (Esther 1:6)

Cord/Chains (Eccles. 12:6)

Crowns (Zech. 6:11)

What things around the sanctuary were made of gold?

Ark box (overlay) (Exod. 25:10, 11)

Plates (Exod. 25:29)

Spoons (Exod. 25:29)

pitchers (Exod. 25:29)

bowls (Exod. 25:29)

Ark rings (Exod. 25:12)

Candlesticks (Exod. 25:31)

Mercy seat (Exod. 25:17)

Curtain hooks (Exod. 26:32)

Two cherubims (Exod. 25:18)

Ephod girdle and chain (Exod. 28:6, 8)

Ark table (overlay) (Exod. 25:23, 24)

Bells (Exod.28:34)

What things in the Bible were made of wood?

Ark (Gen. 6:14)

Hand weapons (Num. 35:18)

Yoke (Jer. 28:13)

Idols/Images (Deut. 29:17)

Table (Exod. 25:23)

Pulpit (Neh. 8:4)

Pillars (Exod. 26:32)

Musical instruments (2 Sam. 6:5)

Altar (Exod. 27:1)

Chariot (Song of Sol. 3:9)

What things in the Bible were made of ivory?

Throne (1 Kings 10:18)

House (1 Kings 22:39)

Palaces (Ps. 45:8)

Benches (Ezek. 27:6)

Horns (Ezek. 27:15)

Beds (Amos 6:4)

What things should be out of your life as written in Ephesians and Colossians? Ephesians 4:31; Colossians 3:8

Bitterness

Evil speaking

Wrath

Malice

Anger

Blasphemy

Clamour

Filty communication

What things did King Solomon ask Hiram to make using brass/bronze?
1 Kings 7:40–45

Two pillars

One large bowl called sea

Two bowls of chapiters

Twelve oxen under

Two network covers for the bowls

Pots

Four hundred pomegranates

Shovels

Ten lavers and bases

Basons

What things did Sheshbazzar bring to Jerusalem from Babylon?
Ezra 1:10–11

Thirty chargers of gold

Thirty basons of gold

One thousand chargers of silver

Four hundred and ten silver basons

Twenty-nine knives

One thousand other vessels

What things mentioned in the Bible were sweet as honey or honeycomb?

Manna (Exod. 16:31)

Fine gold (Ps. 19:10)

Pleasant words (Prov. 16:24)

Lips (Song of Sol. 4:11)

Scroll (Ezek. 3:3)

Book (Rev. 10:9)

What uses for honey in the Bible?
Present or gift (Gen. 43:11)
Food (Deut. 32:13)
Material for a riddle (Judges 14:18)
Tithe offering (2 Chron. 31:5)
Traded in market (Ezek. 27:17)

What furniture of the tabernacle did Moses build? Exodus 37 and 38
The Ark of the Covenant
Table of Showbread
Altar of Incense
Bronze Laver
Golden Lampstand/Candlestick
Altar of Burnt Offering

What equipment (tools) do the four horsemen carry in Revelation 6?
Crown
Bow and arrow
Sword
Balance
Scythe (sickle)

What are the names of gates in Israel?
Sur Gate (2 Kings 11:6)
Upper Gate (2 Kings 15:35)
Kings's Gate (1 Chron. 9:18)
Fountain Gate (2 Chron. 23:5)
Horse Gate (2 Chron. 23:15)
Corner Gate (2 Chron. 26:9)
Valley Gate (2 Chron. 26:9)
Fish Gate (2 Chron. 33:14)
Dung Gate (Neh. 2:13)
Sheep Gate (Neh. 3:1)

What white things can be found in the Bible that are related to animals?

Sheep (Gen. 30:35)

Teeth (Gen. 49:12)

Skin (Lev. 13:4)

Ass (Judges 5:10)

Egg (Job 6:6)

Wool (Ezek. 27:18)

Horse (Zech. 6:3)

Hair (Matt. 5:36)

Chestnut branch (Gen. 30:37)

Basket (Gen. 40:16)

Manna (Exod. 16:31)

Garments (Eccles. 9:8)

Snow (Ps. 68:14)

Raiment (Matt. 28:3)

Fields (John 4:35)

Stone (Rev. 2:17)

Cloud (Rev. 14:14)

Throne (Rev. 20:11)

What black things are found in the Bible?

Hair (Lev. 13:37)

Raven (Song of Sol. 5:11)

Clouds (1 Kings 18:45)

Horse (Zech. 6:2)

Skin (Job 30:30)

Sackcloth (Rev. 6:12)

What blue things are found in the Bible?

Vail/curtain (Exod. 26:31)

Linen (Exod. 28:5)

Robe (Exod. 28:31)

Pomegranates (Exod. 28:33)

Cloth (Num. 4:6)

What red things are found in the Bible?

Skin (Gen. 25:25)

Pottage (Gen. 25:30)

Wine (Gen. 49:12)

Sea (Exod. 15:4)

Ram's skin (Exod. 25:5)

Apparel (Isa. 63:2)

Shield (Nah. 2:3)

Horse (Zech. 6:2)

Sky (Matt. 16:2)

Dragon (Rev. 12:3)

What green things are found in the Bible?

Herbs (Gen. 9:3)

Pastures (Ps. 23:2)

Tree (2 Kings 16:4)

Bed (Song of Sol. 1:16)

Curtains (Esther 1:6)

Grass (Mark 6:39)

What purple and yellow things are found in the Bible?

Vail (Exod. 26:31)

Linen (Exod. 35:6)

Pomegranates (Exod. 39:24)

Cloth (Num. 4:13)

Feathers (Ps. 68:13)

Hair (Song of Sol. 7:5)

What banners and colors of the four tribe leaders of Israel?
Ezekiel 1:10; 10:14; Numbers 2:3, 10, 18, 25

Lion of gold with a scarlet background (Judah—East)

Ox of black on gold background (Ephraim—West)

Face of Man on gold background (Reuben—South)

Eagle of gold on a blue background (Dan—North)

What are the parts of the full armor of God to stand in life's battle?
Ephesians 6:13–17

Belt of Truth

Shield of Faith

Breastplate of Righteousness

Helmet of Salvation

Shoe of Gospel of Peace

Sword of the Spirit

What musical instruments did men in the Bible play?

Cornet/Horn (2 Sam. 6:5)

Pipe (1 Sam. 10:5)

Cymbal (2 Sam. 6:5)

Psaltery/Sackbut (2 Sam. 6:5)

Flute (Dan. 3:7)

Timbrel/tabret/tambourines (2 Sam. 6:5)

Harp (2 Sam. 6:5)

Trumpet (1 Chron. 15:28)

Organ (Gen. 4:21)

Lyre (Isa. 5:11)

What musical instruments were mentioned by David used to praised God? Psalm 150

Trumpet

Strings

Harp

Pipe

Lyre

Cymbals

Timbrel

What musical instrument were played for the people to worship the image King Nebuchadnezzar built? Daniel 3:8–10

Cornet

Psaltery

Flute

Dulcimer

Harp

Sackbut

What things were considered unclean when touched by a carcass?
Wooden vessels (Lev. 11:32)
Oven (Lev. 11:35)
Sack (Lev. 11:32)
Pots (Lev. 11:35)
Raiment (Lev. 11:32)
Fountain or pit of water (Lev. 11:36)
Earthen vessels (Lev. 11:33)
Bed or seat (Lev. 15:4)

The branches of which trees were used to make huts during festivities in Israel? Nehemiah 8:15

Olive
Pine
Myrtle
Palm
Other thick trees

What were Bible-time weapons of wars?
Spears (2 Chron. 26:14)
Shield (2 Chron. 26:14)
Helmets (2 Chron. 26:14)
Javelin (Num. 25:7)
Habergeons (2 Chron. 26:14)
Chariots and horses (Exod. 14:9)
Bow and arrows (2 Kings 13:15)
Buckler (1 Chron. 12:8,9)
Sling and Stones (2 Chron. 26:14)
Armour (2 Chron. 26:14)
Sword (1 Sam. 13:20)

What things did God call "good" in the Bible?

Light (Gen. 1:4)

Dry land and seas (Gen. 1:10)

Vegetation (Gen. 1:12)

Day and night (Gen. 1:18)

Animals of land, sea and air (Gen. 1:21, 25)

Ground (Mark 4:20)

Salt (Mark 9:50)

Gifts unto your children (Luke 11:13)

Wine (John 2:10)

Shepherd (John 10:11)

What natural things in the Bible are described as "goodly?"

Trees (Lev. 23:40)

Mountain (Deut. 3:25)

Peacocks' wings (Job 39: 13)

Cedars (Ps. 80:10)

Fruit (Jer. 11:16)

Vine (Ezek. 17:8)

Horse (Zech. 10:3)

Pearls (Matt. 13:45)

Stones (Luke 21:5)

What man-made things in the Bible are described as "goodly?"

Garment/raiment (Gen. 27:15)

Words (Gen. 49:21)

Houses/tents/castles (Num. 24:5; 31:10)

Cities (Deut. 6:10)

Babylonian garment (Joshua 7:21)

Vessels of the house (2 Chron. 36:10)

Heritage (Ps. 16:6)

Images (idols) (Hosea 10:1)

Apparel (James 2:2)

What "good" things are mentioned in the Bible?

Good years (Gen. 41:35)

Good doctrine (Prov.4:2)

Good and right way (1 Sam. 12:23)

Good day (1 Sam. 25:8)

Good judgement and knowledge (Ps. 119:66)

Good and faithful servant (Matt. 25:21)

Good fight (1 Tim. 6:12)

Good foundation (1 Tim. 6:19)

What good things are found in the promised land? Deuteronomy 8:7–9

Brooks of water	Barley
Pomegranates	Honey
Fountains and springs	Vines
Olive oil	Stones of iron
Wheat	Fig trees
Milk	Brass under hills

What "good" things are found in a farm or on land?

Good goat (Gen. 27:9)

Good ears of corn (Gen. 41:5)

Good dowry (Gen. 30:20)

Good treasure (Deut. 28:12)

Good fruit (figs) (Judges 9:11)

Good tree (2 Kings 3:19)

Good ointment (savour) (Song of Sol. 1:3)

Good smell from grapes (Song of Sol. 2:13)

Good ground (Matt. 13:8)

Good seed (Matt. 13:24)

What things are described as "sweet" in the Bible

Psalmist (2 Sam. 23:1)

Wickedness (Job 20:12)

Clods (Job 21:33)

Pleiades (Job 38:31)

Counsel (Ps. 55:14)

Meditations (Ps. 104:34)

Words (Ps. 119:103)

Accomplished desire
(Prov. 13:19)

Lips (Prov. 16:21)

Bread of deceit (Prov. 20:17)

Sleep (Eccles. 5:12)

Light (Eccles. 11:7)

Voice (Song of Sol. 2:14)

Flowers (Song of Sol. 5:13)

Myrrh (Song of Sol. 5:13)

Mouth (Song of Sol. 5:16)

Melody (Isa. 23:16)

Little Book (Rev. 10:9, 10)

What sweet foods are mentioned in the Bible?

Savour (Gen. 8:21)

Water (Exod. 15:25; Prov. 9:17)

Incense (Exod. 25:6)

Cinnamon (Exod. 30:23)

Spices (Exod. 37:29)

Odour/smell (Lev. 26:31; Isa. 3:24)

Honey/honeycomb (Judges 14:18; Ps. 19:10)

Apple fruit (Song of Sol. 2:3)

Cane (Isa. 43:24)

Wine (Isa. 49:26)

What kinds of wood or trees were used to build things in the Bible?

Gopher/Cypress—Noah's Ark (Gen. 6:14)

Shittim/Acacia—Ark of Covenant (Exod. 25:10)

Olive—Door and post of temple (1 Kings 6:32)

Cedar—House of David (2 Sam. 5:11)

Fir—Musical instrument (2 Sam. 6:5)

Pine (Isa. 60:13)

Oak (Isa. 6:13)

Willow (Ezek. 17:5)

What actual yokes are mentioned in the Bible?

Heifer hath not drawn in the yoke (Deut. 21:3)

Female cow with calf, tie yoke to cart to bring the Ark back to Israelites (1 Sam. 6:7)

Yoke of oxen, hewed in pieces and sent throughout Israel by Saul (1 Sam. 11:7)

Elisha plowing with twelve yoke of oxen when Elijah passed by (1 Kings 19:19)

Job had five hundred yoke of oxen (Job 1:3)

Bullock unaccustomed to the yoke (Jer. 31:18)

I have bought five yoke of oxen (Luke 14:19)

The tongue is compared to what in the Bible?

Pen (Ps. 45:1)

Sharp razor (Ps. 52:2)

Sword (Ps. 64:3)

Choice silver (Prov. 10:20)

Health (Prov. 12:18)

Tree of life (Prov. 15:4)

Bow of lies/deceitful bow (Jer. 9:3; Hosea 7:16)

Arrow shot out (Jer. 9:8)

Fire (Acts 2:3)

Sounding brass, tinkling cymbal (1 Cor. 13:1)

Unruly evil (James 3:8)

What things are found at the "Right Hand" in the Old Testament?

Blood of a ram—Aaron and his sons (Exod. 29:20)

Trumpets—Israelites at Jericho (Judges 7:20)

Oil—Priest (Lev. 14:16, 17)

Blood of lamb—Priest (Lev. 14:25)

Idols on mount of corruption—King Solomon (2 Kings 23:13)

Seat for his mother—King Solomon (1 Kings 2:19)

Dagger—Ehud (Judges 3:21)

Hammer—Jael smote Sisera (Judges 5:26)

Bows and arrows—Saul's brethren (1 Chron. 12:2)

Wise man's heart (Eccles. 10:2)

Arrows (Eze. 39:3)

Cup of the Lord (Hab. 2:16)

What things are found at the "Right Hand" in the New Testament?

Sheep (Matt. 25:33)

Reed (stick) (Matt. 27:29)

Seven stars (Rev. 2:1)

Book sealed with seven seals (Rev. 5:1)

Mark of the Beast (Rev. 13:16)

What offerings did God instruct Moses that Israel could bring?
Exodus 25:1–8

Precious stones or gem

Badger's skin

Fine linen

Shittim wood

Goat's hair

Oil

Ram's skins

Spices

What did God ask Moses to tell the Israelites to offer for the dedication of the altar? Numbers 7:84–89

Silver charger (plate)

Silver bowl full of fine flour mixed with oil

Golden spoon full of incense

Six male goats

One young bull

Two oxen

Six male sheep

Six male lamb

What things are described that ceased at the destruction of Babylon?
Revelation 18:22, 23

Voice of harpers
No craftsman working
Voice of musicians
Sound of a millstone
Voice of pipers
Light of a candle
Voice of trumpeters
Voice of the bridegroom and bride

What merchandise will not be bought or sold at the destruction of Babylon? Revelation 18:12–13

Gold
Vessels of ivory
Silver
Vessels of brass
Pearls
Vessels of iron
Fine linen and silk
Vessels of marble
Precious wood
Chariots

Cinnamon
Fine flour/wheat
Odours
Beast (cattle)/Sheep
Ointments/frankincense
Horses
Wine
Slaves
Oil
Souls of men

What things are hidden by an unnamed person in the Bible?
Hatred with lying lips (Prov. 10:18)
Light (Matt. 5:14)
Treasure (Matt. 13:44)
Bag of the Lord's money (Matt. 25:18, 25)
Secret (Mark 4:22)

What materials were used to make gods in Daniel 5:23?
Silver
Iron
Gold
Wood
Brass
Stone

What stones being rolled are mentioned in the Bible?
Jacob rolled the stone from the well's mouth (Gen. 29:3, 8, 10)
Joshua's men rolled the stone upon the cave's mouth (Joshua10:18)
Saul ordered to roll great stone (1 Sam. 14:33)
Rolled a stone unto the door of the sepulcher (Matt. 27:60)
Angel rolled back the stone from the door (Matt. 28:2)

What stones have a special use mentioned in the Old Testament?
Jacob used as a pillow (Gen. 28:11)
Jacob used to set up a pillar, heap (Gen. 31: 45, 46)
Covering the well where sheep drank (Gen. 29:2)
Zipporah used to cut off foreskin of her son (Exod. 4:25)
Moses sat upon a stone while his hands stayed raised to win the war (Exod. 17:12)
Ten Commandments that God gave to Moses (Exod. 24:12; 34:4)
Precious stone set in the priest's ephod (Exod. 25:7)
Joshua set up twelve stones in the Jordan were the priests stood (Joshua 4:9)
Joshua wrote upon the stones a copy of the Law of Moses (Joshua 8:32)
The Lord cast down great stones from heaven upon Azekah (Joshua 10:11)
Abimelech killed his brothers with one stone (Joshua 9:5, 18)
Samuel set a stone between Mizpeh and Shen and named it Ebenezer (1 Sam. 7:12)
David took five stone, one killed Goliath (1 Sam. 17:40–50)
Shimei cast stones at David and his men (2 Sam. 16:6, 13)

Absalom was cast in a pit and great heaps of stones were laid (2 Sam. 18:17)

Joab killed Amasa at the great stone which is in Gibeon (2 Sam. 20:8)

Solomon brought great stones to be the temple's foundation (1 Kings 5:17)

Elijah built an altar from twelve stones representing the sons of Jacob (1 Kings 18:31)

Stone which the builders refused become the head corner stone (Ps. 118:22)

Stone was cut out of the mountain without hands and broke the image (Dan. 2:34, 35)

Stone was brought and laid upon the mouth of the lion's den (Dan. 6:17)

What stone have a special use mentioned in the New Testament?

Satan tempted Jesus to command these stones be made break (Matt. 4:3)

Would a father give a stone if his son asked for bread (Matt. 7:9)

Jesus' parable about the vineyard, tenant stones his servants (Matt. 21:35)

The builders rejected, the same became the corner stone (Matt. 21:42)

Stone sealing the sepulchre, Jesus' tomb (Matt. 27:66)

Stone never cast at the woman accused of adultery (John 8:7)

Jesus said the stones will cry out if the disciples should hold this peace (Luke 19:40)

Stones never cast at Jesus by the Jews (John 10:31)

Stones cast at Stephen (Acts 7:59)

Stones cast at Paul (Acts 14:19)

What events mentioned in the Bible, at the time of it's writing, were described by the words, "unto this day?"

Joseph made it a law over the land of Egypt (Gen. 47:26)

God which fed me [Joseph] all my life long (Gen. 48:15)

The Lord separated the tribe of Levi to bear the Ark of the Covenant and minister (Deut. 10:8)

Rahab the harlot and her father's household dwelleth in Israel (Joshua 6:25)

Joshua burnt Ai and made it an heap/desolation for ever (Joshua 8:28)

Joshua laid great stones in the cave's mouth (Joshua 10:27)

Solomon levied a tribute of bond service (1 Kings 9:21)

Almug wood has never been imported or seen since that day (1 Kings 10:12)

Elisha healed the waters (2 Kings 2:22)

Jonadab commanded his sons not to drink wine (Jer. 35:14)

What structures or monuments were built and exist "unto this day" at the time of the Bible writing?

Jacob set a pillar upon her grave (Gen. 35:20)

God destroyed Pharaoh's army (Deut. 11:4)

No man knoweth the location of the sepulcher of Moses (Deut. 34:6)

Joshua set up twelve stones in the midst of the Jordan (Joshua 4:9)

Joshua cast the carcass of the King of Ai at the gate and raised a great heap of stones (Joshua 8:29)

Hebron became the inheritance of Caleb the Kenezite (Joshua 14:14)

The Lord hath driven out great nations and no man hath been able to stand before you (Joshua 23:9)

No such deed was done or seen from the day Israel came out of Egypt (Judges 19:30)

Hast made thee a name, set signs and wonders in the land of Egypt (Jer. 32:20)

What was cursed in the Bible?

Serpent (Gen. 3:14)

Ground/earth (Gen. 3:17)

Basket/store (Deut. 28:17)

Fruit of thy body (Deut. 28:18)

Fruit of the land (Deut. 28:18)

Man/people (Jer. 11:3)

Fig tree (Mark 11:21)

What "precious" things were mentioned in the Bible?

Ointment (1 Kings 20:13)

Jewels (2 Chron. 20:25)

Stones (2 Sam. 12:30)

Onyx (Job 28:16)

Seed (Ps. 126:6)

Substance (Prov. 1:13)

Riches (Prov. 24:4)

Corner Stone (Isa. 28:16)

Vessels (Dan. 11:8)

Clothes (Ezek. 27:20)

Fruit (James 5:7)

Blood of Christ (1 Pet. 1:19)

Sons of Zion (Lam. 4:2)

Faith (2 Pet. 1:1)

Promises (2 Pet. 1:4)

What divine instructions were given on how the Ark of the Lord would be returned to Israel? 1 Samuel 6:7

Get a new cart ready

Put the Ark of the Lord in the Cart

Hitch two never-been-yoked cows to the cart

Send gold guilt offering with the Ark

Take their calves away and pen them up

Keep watching it on its way back

Animals

What descriptions are given of the 1st beast in Daniel's vision? Daniel 7:3–4

Came up from the sea

It was lifted up from the earth

Was like a lion

Made stand upon the feet as a man

Had eagle's wings

A man's heart was given to it

Wings thereof were plucked

What descriptions are given of the 2nd beast in Daniel's vision? Daniel 7:3, 5

Came up from the sea

Like to a bear

It raised up itself on one side

It had three ribs in the mouth between the teeth

Arise, devour much flesh

What descriptions are given of the 3rd beast in Daniel's vision? Daniel 7:3, 6

Came up from the sea

Like a leopard

Upon the back of it four wings of a fowl

Had also four heads

Dominion was given to it

What animals used as symbols in Bible Prophecy?

Horse (Job 39:19)

Serpent (Rev. 12:9)

Dragon (Isa. 27:1)

Wolf (Matt. 7:15)

Lamb (John 1:29)

Dove (Mark 1:10)

Lion (Rev. 5:4–9)

Ram (Dan. 8:20)

Bear (Prov. 28:15)

Goat (Dan. 8:21)

Leopard (Dan. 7:6)

What guidelines did God give for creatures that are good to eat? Leviticus 11

Split hoof

Winged insect that walk on four legs

Chew the cud

Insect with joint legs for hopping

Fish with fins

Insect that does not creep

Fish with scales

What unclean animals are listed in Leviticus 11?

Camel

Rats

Coney

Lizard

Rabbit

Reptiles

Pig

Snail

Mouse

Mole

What unclean birds are listed in Leviticus 11? (NIV)

 Eagle

 Gull and Hawk

 Vulture

 Cormorant

 Kite

 Swan and Pelican

 Raven

 Stork and Keron

 Owl

 Lapwing and Bat

What various types of insects are mentioned in the Bible?

 Ant (Prov. 6:6; 30:25)

 Bee (Judges 14:8)

 Grasshopper (Judges 6:5)

 Beetle (Lev. 11:22)

 Lice (Exod. 8:16)

 Caterpillar/Worm (1 Kings 8:37/Exod. 16:20)

 Locust (Exod. 10:4)

 Flea/Hornet (1 Sam. 24:14)

 Moth (Job 13:28)

 Fly/Gnat (1 Sam. 24:14)

What animals did Isaiah see in his vision of the new Earth? Isaiah 11:6–8

 Wolf

 Cow/Calf/Ox

 Lamb

 Bear

 Leopard

 Asp/Cockatrice

 Lion

What bird are mentioned in the Bible?

Chicken (Matt.23:37)

Cock/Rooster (Mark 14:30)

Quail (Num. 11:31)

Dove (Gen. 8:8)

Raven (Gen. 8:7)

Eagles/Ossifrage/Osprey
(Lev. 11:13)

Swallows (Prov. 26:2)

Owls (Ps. 102:6)

Pelican (Ps. 102:6)

Peacocks/Ostrich (Job 39:13)

Hawk/Cuckow (Lev. 11:16)

Sparrow (Matt. 10:29–31)

What are God's description of the behemoth he created?
Job 40:15–24 (KJV, NIV)

I made the behemoth

He eats grass like an ox

Has great strength in his body, stomach muscles are powerful

His tail stands strong like a cedar tree

His bones are as strong as bronze

His legs muscles are very strong like iron bars

He lies and hides under shade of the lotus plants

He lives under the willow trees that grow near the river and swamp

He is not afraid of Jordan River floods and splashes on his face

No one can blind his eyes and capture him in a trap

What are God's description of leviathan? Job 41:1–34 (NKJV)

Sparks of fire shoots out of mouth when sneezing

His rows or scales are his pride

Smoke goes out of his nostrils, breath kindles coals

Strength dwells in his neck

Folds of his flesh are joined together

His heart is as hard as stone/millstone

When he raises himself up, the mighty are afraid

Sword, spear, dart, or javelin cannot avail and make him flee

He regards iron as straw and bronze as rotten wood

Makes the deep sea like a boiling pot of ointment

Nothing on earth like him

What animals are found in groups of twelve in the Bible?

Twelve oxen (Num. 7:3)

Twelve goats for offering (Num. 7:87)

Twelve bullocks for offering (Num. 7:87)

Twelve rams for offering (Num. 7:87)

Elisha plowing with twelve yoke of oxen (1 Kings 19:19)

Twelve lions in the statue in Solomon's throne (1 Kings 10:20)

What animals come in groups of two in the Bible?

Goats (Gen. 27:9)

Lambs (Exod. 29:38)

Turtledoves (Lev. 5:7)

Pigeons (Lev. 5:7)

Ram (Lev. 8:2)

Unclean animals, male and female (Gen. 6:19)

Bullocks (Num. 28:11)

Lions (2 Chron. 9:18)

Sparrows (Matt. 10:29)

Fishes (Matt. 14:17)

Eagles (Rev. 12:14)

In what instances are 100 animals referenced in the Bible?

100 sheep, food supply for Solomon's table (1 Kings 4:22–23)

100 rams sacrificed as burnt offering (2 Chron. 29:32)

100 bulls offered at God's temple dedication (Ezra 6:17)

100 sheep, one lost in Jesus' parable (Luke 15:4)

Satan

What are the other names of Satan?

Lucifer (Isa. 14:12)

Beelzebub (Matt. 12:24)

Apollyon (Rev. 9:11)

Abaddon (Rev. 9:11)

What words or terms used in the Bible describe Satan?

Son of the morning (Isa. 14:12)

Anointed cherub (Ezek. 28:12–15)

Tempter (Matt. 4:3)

Prince of the devils, devil (Matt. 4:8, 11)

Wicked one (Matt. 13:19)

Prince/god of this world (John 12:31; 2 Cor. 4:4)

Prince of the power of the air (Eph. 2:2)

Accuser of brethren (Rev. 12:9–10)

Dragon, great dragon (Rev. 12:9, 12)

Old serpent (Rev. 20:2)

What are names of gods found in the Old Testament?

Asherah, Ashtoreth, Amon—Canaanites, Thebes (Jer. 46:25; Judges 6:25)

Ashima, Rimmon—Syrian (2 Kings 17:30)

Baal Chemosh—Moabites (Isa. 46:1)

Baal-Zebub—Philistines (2 Kings 1:2, 3)

Dagon—Philistines (2 Kings 1:2, 3)

Merodach, Marduk—Babylonians (Jer 50:2)

Molech, Milcom—Ammonites (1 Kings 11:5, 33)

Nebo, Nergal—Babylonians (Amos 5:26; Isa. 46:1; 2 Kings 17:30)

Nibhaz, Tartak—Avites (2 Kings 17:31)

Tammuz—Babylonians and Samarians (2 Kings 17:30; Ezek. 8:14)

What animals or things related to animals are used to describe Satan?

Leviathan (Isa. 27:1)

Little horn (Dan. 8:9)

Roaring lion (1 Pet. 5:8)

Great dragon (Rev. 12:9)

Old serpent (Rev. 12:9)

Beast (Rev. 14:9)

What names used to describe Satan illustrate what he does on this earth?

Accuser (Rev. 12:10)

Ruler of this world (Eph. 6:12)

Deceiver (Rev. 12:9)

Tempter (Matt. 4:3)

Enemy (Matt. 13:39)

Thief (John 10:10)

Father of Lies, Liar (John 8:44)

Wicked one (Eph. 6:16)

Murderer (John 8:44)

What does Lucifer say he will do, according to Isaiah 14:13, 14?: "I Will…"

… ascend into heaven

… exalt my throne above the stars of God

… sit also upon the mount of the congregation

… ascend above the heights of the clouds

… be like the Most High

What are six abodes of Satan?

Mountain of God (Ezek. 28:14)

Garden of Eden, before his fall (Ezek. 28:13)

The air (Eph. 2:2)

Earth, mid-tribulation (Rev 12:7–12)

Abyss (Rev 9:1–11)

Lake of Fire (Rev 19:20)

When were unclean spirits cast out?

Man with unclean spirits that entered into swine (Mark 5:13)

Daugther of syrophoenician woman (Mark 7:25)

Man inside the synagogue at Capernaum (Luke 4:33)

Several unclean spirits at the coast of Tyre (Luke 6:18)

Unclean spirit cast out from a boy (Luke 9:42)

Peter healed and cast out unclean spirits (Acts 5:16)

Unclean spirits came out like frogs (Rev. 16:13)

TEACH Services, Inc.
P U B L I S H I N G

We invite you to view the complete
selection of titles we publish at:
www.TEACHServices.com

We encourage you to write us
with your thoughts about this,
or any other book we publish at:
info@TEACHServices.com

TEACH Services' titles may be purchased in
bulk quantities for educational, fund-raising,
business, or promotional use.
bulksales@TEACHServices.com

Finally, if you are interested in seeing
your own book in print, please contact us at:
publishing@TEACHServices.com
We are happy to review your manuscript at no charge.

CPSIA information can be obtained
at www.ICGtesting.com
Printed in the USA
LVOW03s0305241017
553516LV00004B/5/P

9 781479 608133